A quick beginners' course
in spoken Russian for
holidaymakers and business
people

Course writer
Nicholas J. Brown
Lecturer in Russian
School of Slavonic
and East European Studies
University of London

Producer: Katherine Flower

BBC Books

Get by in Russian
A BBC Radio course
First broadcast in Spring 1990

Published to accompany a series of programmes
prepared in consultation with the Continuing Education
Advisory Council

Acknowledgments
The author is grateful for the assistance of Kathy Flower,
Philippa Goodrich, Sarah Hoggett, Keith Crawford and
Suzanne Webber at the BBC; and to Irina Panasyuk, Galya,
Gena, Lena, Lyosha, Margarita Yakovlyevna, Misha, Sasha and
some two hundred other Soviet citizens.

Illustrations by Peter Clark

Published by BBC Books, a division of BBC Enterprises Ltd,
Woodlands, 80 Wood Lane, London W12 0TT

ISBN 0 563 21495 3
First published in 1990
© Nicholas J. Brown 1990

Printed and bound in England by
Ebenezer Baylis & Son Ltd, The Trinity Press, Worcester
This book is set in 10 and 11 point Helvetica by Typesetters Ltd,
Hertford, Hertfordshire
Cover printed by Richard Clay Ltd, Norwich

Contents

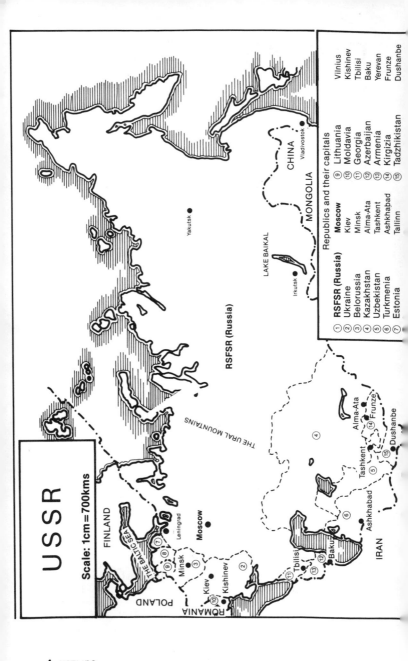

USSR

Scale: 1cm=700kms

FINLAND
POLAND
ROMANIA
THE BALTIC SEA
Leningrad
Moscow
Minsk
Kiev
Kishinev
Tbilisi
Baku
Ashkhabad
Tashkent
Alma-Ata
Frunze
Dushanbe
IRAN
THE URAL MOUNTAINS
RSFSR (Russia)
Yakutsk
Irkutsk
LAKE BAIKAL
Vladivostok
MONGOLIA
CHINA

Republics and their capitals

① RSFSR (Russia)	**Moscow**
② Ukraine	Kiev
③ Belorussia	Minsk
④ Kazakhstan	Alma-Ata
⑤ Uzbekistan	Tashkent
⑥ Turkmenia	Ashkhabad
⑦ Estonia	Tallinn
⑧ Lithuania	Vilnius
⑨ Moldavia	Kishinev
⑩ Georgia	Tbilisi
⑪ Azerbaijan	Baku
⑫ Armenia	Yerevan
⑬ Kirgizia	Frunze
⑭ Tadzhikistan	Dushanbe

4 четыре

About 'Get by in Russian'

Get by in Russian is a basic 'survival kit' to help you manage without your Intourist guide and let you get away from the English-only tourist track. The book can be used on its own, but for best results you need the accompanying two cassettes.

The conversations were specially recorded in Moscow and Leningrad – in streets, flats, shops, hotels and cafés – so that you get used to hearing authentic Russian right from the start.

The Russian (Cyrillic) alphabet may seem a daunting hurdle at first, but you will find that learning it is an important part of 'getting by'. In the USSR street signs, station names, notices and so on are given only in Russian letters. In this book we give Russian words in both Cyrillic and English letters but we recommend that you try to get used to reading Cyrillic as soon as possible.

Welcome to the USSR (CCCP)

The USSR is by far the largest country in the world. It is one-sixth of the world's land surface, two and a half times the size of China, ninety times the size of Great Britain. It is divided into fifteen republics, of which the best known is Russia. Many foreigners use the name Russia for the whole country but this usage is offensive to the large number of its citizens who are not Russians. It is better to say the Soviet Union – **Совётский Союз** [Sa-vyét-skee Sa-yóos] in Russian. The population of 280 000 000 is made up of over a hundred different nationalities, all with their own languages. The fifteen republics – Russia (or RSFSR), Ukraine, Latvia, Lithuania, Estonia, Georgia, Uzbekistan, Armenia etc. – are named after the fifteen historically most important nationalities. Only about a half of all Soviet citizens are ethnic Russians, but the Russian language is a *lingua franca* for everbody.

The country is so big that when it is nine in the morning in Moscow, it is already seven in the evening on the Kamchatka peninsula in the Soviet Far East. Yet if you travel on the Trans-Siberian railway from Moscow to Vladivostok, right across Siberia, you never leave the republic called Russia; the other fourteen republics are all in the west and south of the country.

Although the Russian Empire of the tsars started to industrialise at the end of the nineteenth century, the country was a very long way behind Britain, France and Germany when the February and October Revolutions of 1917 swept away the monarchy and the social order described in the works of Chekhov and Tolstoy. From the misery and defeat of the First World War, Russia was plunged into the upheavals of Lenin's huge experiment, then the trauma of the 1918–20 Civil War, the years of Stalin's ruthless dictatorship and the holocaust of Hitler's 1941 invasion. After 1945 the European part of the country had to be rebuilt, and the Cold War between the 'Iron Curtain' countries and the West meant that industry and defence had to be developed as quickly as possible – if necessary, at the expense of individual freedom and comfort. Only in the late 1980s, after forty years of peace and thirty-five years since the end of Stalin's reign of terror, are the USSR's leaders beginning to feel secure, more at ease with their neighbours (especially China), less suspicious of their own citizens.

Western visitors have tended to find the country rather drab on the surface but have always commented on the friendliness of the Russians and their eagerness to meet foreigners – often their only source of contact with the exotic world outside, since even now a trip to the West is almost impossible for the vast majority.

Despite their Revolution, the Russians always give the impression of being a conservative people who believe in such traditional things as family life, entertaining friends at home and a sense of community. They are very proud of their language and its world-class literature. Despite 1917, twentieth-century Russian is in all essentials the same language as Dostoevsky and Tolstoy used a hundred years ago. You will also find a great degree of uniformity across the Soviet Union: dialect variations are surprisingly small for such a large country and will not cause the foreign learner problems.

The Russian (Cyrillic) Alphabet

The Cyrillic alphabet was invented around 860 AD, possibly by St Cyril, a Macedonian monk. It is based on Greek.

To 'get by' in Russian – to read signs and street names, for example – you will need to know this alphabet. It is not difficult to learn and, apart from some minor exceptions (see page 12), words are pronounced as they are written. In this book all the Cyrillic in the first three units is also given in English letters; in the other three units, all new words are given in both Cyrillic and English letters, as are parts of the dialogues, so that you can check your pronunciation and progress. To make things easier, when showing the pronunciation in English letters, we have also divided the words up into syllables.

We'll do the five easy letters first:

CAPITAL	SMALL	PRONUNCIATION
A	a	a as in father
K	к	k as in kangaroo
M	м	m as in man
T	т	t as in tan
O	o	o as in bottle (*but* pronounced a when unstressed, i.e. with no stress mark '; see page 12)

Examples

так	[tak]	'so'
там	[tam]	'there'
как	[kak]	'how'
кто-то	[któ-ta]	'somebody'

Then the seven letters which look like English letters but have different sounds:

В	в	v as in vet
Е	е	ye as in yes
Н	н	n as in never
Р	р	r as in error (rolled as in Scots English)
С	с	s as in sit
У	у	oo as in boot
Х	х	h pronounced like the ch in Scots loch or German Bach

Examples

нет	[nyet]	no
Москва́	[Mask-vá]	Moscow
метро́	[mye-tró]	metro, underground
Ве́ра	[Vyé-ra]	Vera
вам	[vam]	to you
у́тро	[oó-tra]	morning
о́н	[ón]	he
она́	[a-ná]	she
сестра́	[sye-strá]	sister
рестора́н	[rye-sta-rán]	restaurant
са́хар	[sá-har]	sugar

Next, 13 letters which look unfamiliar but have familiar sounds:

Б	б	b as in bet
Г	г	g as in get
Д	д	d as in debt
Ё	ё	yo as in yonder
З	з	z as in zoo
И	и	ee as in eel
Й	й	y as in boy
Л	л	l as in people
П	п	p as in pet
Ф	ф	f as in fat
Э	э	e as in fed
Ю	ю	yoo as in universe
Я	я	ya as in yak

stuz

Examples

→ | Аэрофло́т | [A-e-ra-flót] | Aeroflot |
|---|---|---|
| Байка́л | [Bay-kál] | Lake Baikal |
| где | [gdye] | where |
| да | [da] | yes |
| до свида́ния | [da-svee-dá-nee-ya] | goodbye |
| алле́ | [a-llyó] | hello (on phone) |
| йли | [ée-lee] | or |
| кио́ск | [kee-ósk] | kiosk |
| Ле́нин | [Lyé-neen] | Lenin |
| парк | [park] | park |
| Пра́вда | [Práv-da] | 'Pravda'/truth |
| Росси́я | [Ra-ssée-ya] | Russia |
| телефо́н | [tye-lye-fón] | telephone |
| ко́фе | [kó-fye] | coffee |
| футбо́л | [foot-ból] | football |
| Югосла́вия | [Yoo-ga-slá-vee-ya] | Yugoslavia |
| я не зна́ю | [ya nye zná-yoo] | I don't know |

Lastly, we have eight letters which take a little longer to learn:

Ж	ж	zh pronounced like the s in pleasure
Ц	ц	ts as in its
Ч	ч	ch as in check
Ш	ш	sh as in shall
Щ	щ	shsh as in Welsh sheep (longer and softer than ш)
Ъ	ъ	a rare letter, called the hard sign, which sounds like a very brief pause
Ы	ы	i as in bit, but with the tip of the tongue a little further back
Ь	ь	y as in canyon. This letter, called the soft sign, combines with the consonant to its left and makes it soft. So нь

sounds like the ny in ca<u>ny</u>on, with the [n] and [y] pronounced simultaneously. Always pronounce it like the 'y' in ca<u>ny</u>on, never as the 'y' in 'd<u>y</u>e'.

Examples

дру́жба	[dro͞ozh-ba]	friendship
гости́ница	[ga-ste͞e-nee-tsa]	hotel
чай	[chay]	tea
большо́й	[baly-shóy]	big
бо́рщ	[borshsh]	beetroot soup
объявле́ние	[ab-ya-vlyé-nee-ye]	announcement
сын	[sin]	son
есть	[yesty]	there is
пять	[pyaty]	five
ваш *ва ша*	[vash]	your
щи	[shshee]	<u>cabbage soup</u>

капуста

Exercise 1

Practise reading the following words, which you will meet again in the units and which contain all the letters except the rare hard sign ъ. Listen to the cassette and check your pronunciation in the answers at the end of the book.

спаси́бо	'thank you'
два ко́фе	'two coffees'
четы́ре	'four'
я слу́шаю	'I'm listening'
Где музе́й?	'Where's the museum?'
моро́женое	'ice cream'
Э́то хорошо́	'That's good'
о́н придёт	'he'll come'
~~това́рищ~~	'comrade' *ДРУГ*
двена́дцать	'twelve' (12)

Stress

Almost all Russian words have a heavy stress on one syllable. For example, the name **Влади́мир** (Vladimir) is pronounced [Vla-dée-meer], with a heavy stress on the second syllable, like Belínda (not Bélinda). In this book the stress is marked ' on Russian words, whether they are written in Cyrillic or in English letters. You should try to learn the place of the stress when you learn the word.

Except in dictionaries and books for foreigners, Russians do not print the stress, so you will often have to read words whose stress you do not know; the safest thing is to read them with no stress at all, syllable by syllable.

Differences between spelling and speaking

When Russian is spoken at normal speed you will notice some differences between spelling and pronunciation. Listen carefully to the cassettes and compare the Cyrillic spelling with our representation of the pronunciation in English letters.

The most obvious one is the pronounciation of unstressed **o** as [a].

óн   [ón]   he
она́   [a-ná] she

The **уй** in the middle of **пожа́луйста** 'please' is often omitted, giving [pa-zhál-sta].

The first **в** in **Здра́вствуйте** 'Hello' is never pronounced, so it's [Zdrá-stvooy-tye];

Что́ 'what' is pronounced [shtó] (not [chtó]).

Sometimes, for example at the ends of words:

б	[b]	is pronounced	[p]
в	[v]	is pronounced	[f]
г	[g]	is pronounced	[k]
д	[d]	is pronounced	[t]
ж	[zh]	is pronounced	[sh]
з	[z]	is pronounced	[s]

Don't worry about trying to remember all of these.
You will not be misunderstood if you simply
pronounce words as they are written.

Exercise 2

Try reading these common signs, then compare
your pronunciation with the cassette and the
answers at the back of the book.

Sign	Translation
БАР	BAR
БУФЕ́Т	SNACKBAR
ГОСТИ́НИЦА	HOTEL
ЗАКРЫ́ТО (a)	CLOSED
ЗА́НЯТО	OCCUPIED
ЗАПРЕЩЕНО́	FORBIDDEN
ИНТУРИ́СТ	INTOURIST
КА́ССА	CASHDESK/TICKET OFFICE
К СЕБЕ́	PULL
МЕ́СТО ДЛЯ КУРЕ́НИЯ	SMOKING PERMITTED HERE
НЕ КУРИ́ТЬ	NO SMOKING
ОТ СЕБЯ́	PUSH
ПАРИКМА́ХЕРСКАЯ	HAIRDRESSER/ BARBER
ПО́ЧТА	POST OFFICE
РАЗМЕ́Н де́нег money	COIN CHANGER (machine in metro stations)
РЕМО́НТ	CLOSED FOR REPAIRS
РЕСТОРА́Н	RESTAURANT
СВОБО́ДНО	UNOCCUPIED/FREE
СТО́П	STOP
СТОЯ́НКА ТАКСИ́	TAXI STAND
ТУАЛЕ́Т	TOILET

Russian words in English letters ('transcription')

The letters in our transcription system are to be read as in English, but be careful with the following ones:

ee always as in meet
  [tak-sée] 'taxi'
i is like the i in bit but with the tongue tip a little further back
  [vi] 'you'
oo always as in boot
  [mye-nyóo] 'menu'
r is always rolled as in Scottish English
  [rye-sta-rán] restaurant
sh as in shut
  [vash] 'your'
  [baly-shóy] 'big'
shsh as in Welsh sheep – a long soft sh sound
  [bórshsh] 'beetroot soup'
ts as in its
  [stán-tsi-ya] 'metro station'
y after a consonant or at the beginning of a
  syllable is pronounced as in yes:
  [Dyá-dya Vá-nya] 'Uncle Vanya'
  [yesty] 'there is'
  [nyet] 'no'
  After a vowel, pronounce it as in boy
  [móy] 'my'
  [moo-zyéy] 'museum'
  [Dáy-tye] 'Give!'
zh is pronounced like s in pleasure
  [pa-zhál-sta] 'please'

ВРЕ́МЯ (handwritten)

1 Greetings

sweets — КОНФЕ́ТЫ (handwritten)
Ka (one sweet (handwritten)

Key expressions

Hello	**Здра́вствуйте** [Zdrá-stvooy-tye – the first **в** is *not* pronounced] **Здра́вствуй** [Zdrá-stvooy – used when speaking to a close friend or child]
Goodbye	**До свида́ния** [Da svee-dá-nee-ya]
Please (also 'Don't mention it', replying to 'Thank you')	**Пожа́луйста** [Pa-zhál-sta] (Note the unstressed o pronounced as [a])
Thank you	**Спаси́бо** [Spa-sée-ba]
1	**оди́н** [a-deén]
2	**два** [dva]
3	**три** [tree]
4	**четы́ре** [chye-tí-rye]

Conversations

1 Saying hello

MAN **Здравствуйте![1]***
[Zdrá-stvooy-tye]

WOMAN **Здравствуйте!**
[Zdrá-stvooy-tye]

* See the Explanations section.

2 Two friends say hello

SASHA **Здравствуй[1], Лёша.**
[Zdrá-stvooy, Lyó-sha]

LYOSHA **Здравствуй, Саша.**
[Zdrá-stvooy, Sá-sha]

3 Saying goodbye

MAN **До свидания[2].**
[Da svee-dá-nee-ya]

WOMAN **До свидания.**
[Da svee-dá-nee-ya]

4 Aspirin, please

CUSTOMER **Аспирин, пожалуйста[3].**
[A-spee-reén, pa-zhál-sta]

CHEMIST **Пожалуйста[3].**
[Pa-zhál-sta]

5 Saying thank you in a shop

CUSTOMER **Спасибо[4].**
[Spa-seé-ba]

ASSISTANT **Пожалуйста[3].**
[Pa-zhál-sta]

6 Ordering a coffee

WAITER **Я вас слушаю.***
[Ya vas sloó-sha-yoo]

*This phrase is often used by waiters and shop assistants to show they are ready to serve you. It means literally, 'I'm listening to you'.

CUSTOMER	**Оди́н ко́фе, пожа́луйста.**
	[A-de'en kó-fye, pa-zhál-sta]
WAITER	**Пожа́луйста.**
	[Pa-zhál-sta]

7 Ordering two coffees

WAITER	**Я вас слу́шаю.**
	[Ya vas sloo-sha-yoo]
CUSTOMER	**Два ко́фе, пожа́луйста.**
	[Dva kó-fye, pa-zhál-sta]
WAITER	**Пожа́луйста.**
	[Pa-zhál-sta]

8 Ordering four coffees

WAITER	**Я вас слу́шаю.**
	[Ya vas sloo-sha-yoo]
CUSTOMER	**Четы́ре ко́фе, пожа́луйста.**
	[Chye-ti-rye kó-fye, pa-zhál-sta]
WAITER	**Возьми́те, пожа́луйста.***
	[Vazy-mee-tye, pa-zhál-sta]

*Take (them), please.

9 Ordering a tea

WAITER	**Я вас слу́шаю.**
	[Ya vas sloo-sha-yoo]
CUSTOMER	**Оди́н чай, пожа́луйста.**
	[A-de'en chay, pa-zhál-sta]
WAITER	**Пожа́луйста.**
	[Pa-zhál-sta]

Word List

ко́фе [kó-fye]	coffee
чай [chay]	tea
я [ya]	I
я (вас) слу́шаю	I'm listening (to you)
[ya (vas) sloo-sha-yoo]	

Explanations

1 Greetings

Здра́вствуйте [Zdrá-stvooy-tye] (literally, 'be healthy'). This is the commonest greeting at any time of day. It's a long word, probably the longest one you have to know in Russian, but you can use it to greet anybody, anywhere. Note that if the person you are speaking to is a friend, a child or a relative, you say

Здра́вствуй [Zdrá-stvooy]
without the final **-те** [-tye].

Good evening **До́брый ве́чер** [Dó-bri vyé-chyer]. You can use this from about 6 pm until midnight. **До́брый** [dó-bri] means 'good' or 'kind' and **ве́чер** [vyé-chyer] means 'evening'.

Good morning **До́брое у́тро** [Dó-bra-ye óo-tra]. As an alternative to **Здра́вствуйте**, you can use **До́брое у́тро** until midday. **У́тро** [óo-tra] means 'morning' and **до́брое** [dó-bra-ye] is a form of the word **до́брый** [dó-bri] ('good' or 'kind').

Good day **До́брый день** [Dó-bri dyeny]. You will also hear this alternative to **Здра́вствуйте**. **День** [dyeny] means 'day'. There is no Russian word for 'afternoon', so this is the one to use between midday and 6pm.

2 Goodbye

До свида́ния [da svee-dá-nee-ya]. Literally, this means 'until meeting'. The word **до** 'until' is usually pronounced without stress, which is why the letter o sounds like [a] (see the pronunciation guide on page 12).

3 Please/Don't mention it/Here you are/Please do

Пожа́луйста [pa-zhál-sta] or, in more careful speech, [pa-zhá-loo-sta].
If you decide to learn only half a dozen Russian words, make this word for 'please' one of them. Put

it in all your requests. Russians do not normally expect foreign visitors to know any Russian; use **пожа́луйста** and the stony-faced official might make an attempt at a smile.

Пожа́луйста also means 'Don't mention it' or 'You're welcome'. If someone says 'Thank you', **спаси́бо** [spa-see-ba], to you, you should reply **Пожа́луйста**, 'Don't mention it'. So the word for 'please' you learnt above is doubly useful.

You also use the word **пожа́луйста** when you give something to somebody ('Here you are') or give permission to do something ('Please do', 'Go ahead').

4 Thank you

Спаси́бо [spa-see-ba] is, of course, a vital word. It has religious origins: **спаси́** [spa-see] means 'save' and **бо** comes from **бог** [bok], 'God' – 'May God save (you)'. But it is now used by all Russians, atheists included, to mean 'thank you'.

Exercises

1 Reading practice

(a)

(b)

(c)

(d)

(e)

(f)

(g)

ПРАВДА

(h)

2 Say hello to **Ива́н Петро́вич** [Ee-ván Pye-tró-veech], whom you are meeting for the first time.

3 Say hello to your old friend Sasha (using the familiar form).

4 Play the part of the customer

WAITER	**Я вас слу́шаю.**
CUSTOMER	(Hello. Three coffees, please.)
WAITER	**Пожа́луйста.**
CUSTOMER	(Thank you)
WAITER	**Пожа́луйста.**

WAITER	**Я вас слу́шаю.**
CUSTOMER	(One tea, please) *оди́н уай п-а*
WAITER	**Пожа́луйста.**
CUSTOMER	(Thank you)
WAITER	**Пожа́луйста.**

5 Read these words and check your pronunciation with the cassette:

(a) **оди́н, два, три, чай, ко́фе, четы́ре, спаси́бо, пожа́луйста, До́брый день, До́брое у́тро, До свида́ния, Здра́вствуйте.**

(b) **Москва́, во́дка, Ло́ндон, Чайко́вский, Достое́вский.**

(c) Here are some Russian names transcribed according to their pronunciation – do you recognise them? The traditional English spellings, and their Cyrillic spellings are given in the exercise key. [Tal-stóy], [Gar-ba-chyóf], [Pa-styer-nák], [Sal-zhe-née-tsin], [Hroo-shshyóf], [Póosh-keen], [Pra-kó-fyyef].

Worth knowing

Russian drinks

Everyone has heard of the strong Russian drink called **вóдка** [vót-ka], though few people know that its name comes from the word **водá** [va-dá] which means 'water'. Among non-alcoholic drinks, the most popular is of course **чай** [chay] 'tea', which is usually served in a thin glass held in a glass-holder (often decorated). An inch of very strong brew is poured into the glass from a small china teapot (**чáйник** [cháy-neek]) and the glass is then filled with boiling water from a kettle or **самовáр** [sa-ma-vár]. Samovars, which are water heaters, not teapots, traditionally used charcoal but modern ones are all electric.

No Russian ever puts milk in tea, but your glass (**стакáн** [sta-kán]) may come with a slice of lemon (**с лимóном** [s lee-mó-nam] 'with lemon'). Lemons are, however, a luxury in Russia and most Russians simply flavour their tea with large lumps of slow-dissolving sugar. Sometimes in Russian homes the tea is accompanied by a small saucer of home-made jam (**варéнье** [va-ryé-nyye]) which you eat with a spoon.

Coffee is also popular but very expensive (a kilo costs 20 roubles, or about two days' pay, when it's available). Ground or instant coffee makes a good present to take with you to the USSR.

2 Buying things

Key expressions

Excuse (me)	**Простите** [Pra-stée-tye]
How much/How many	**Сколько** [Skóly-ka]
How much does it cost?	**Сколько стоит?** [Skóly-ka stó-eet?]
How much do they cost?	**Сколько стоят?** [Skóly-ka stó-yat?]
Could you repeat, please?	**Повторите, пожалуйста** [Pa-fta-rée-tye, pa-zhál-sta]
Show (me)	**Покажите** [Pa-ka-zhí-tye]
One rouble	**Один рубль** [A-dée n roobly]
Two roubles	**Два рубля** [Dva roo-blyá]
Five roubles	**Пять рублей** [Pyaty roo-blyéy]
One kopeck	**Одна копейка** [Ad-ná ka-pyéy-ka]
Two kopecks	**Две копейки** [Dvye ka-pyéy-kee]
Five kopecks	**Пять копеек** [Pyaty ka-pyé-yek]
6	**шесть** [shesty]
7	**семь** [syemy]
8	**восемь** [vó-syemy]
9	**девять** [dyé-vyaty]
10	**десять** [dyé-syaty]

Thank you very much	**Спасибо большое**
	[Spa-see-ba baly-shó-ye]
Good/OK	**Хорошо** [Ha-ra-shó]

Conversations

1 Counting to ten

CHILD **Один** [a-deen], **два** [dva], **три** [tree], **четыре** [chye-tí-rye], **пять** [pyaty], **шесть** [shesty], **семь** [syemy], **восемь** [vó-syemy], **девять** [dyé-vyaty], **десять** [dyé-syaty].

2 Asking the price

CUSTOMER **Сколько?**
[Skóly-ka]

ASSISTANT **Сорок пять[1]. Сорок пять копеек[7].**
[Só-rak pyaty. Só-rak pyaty ka-pyé-yek]

CUSTOMER **Спасибо большое.**
[Spa-see-ba baly-shó-ye]

ASSISTANT **Пожалуйста.**
[Pa-zhál-sta]

3 Asking how much it is

CUSTOMER **Сколько это[2] стоит?**
[Skóly-ka é-ta stó-eet?]

TRADER **Тридцать пять.**
[Tree-tsaty pyaty]

CUSTOMER **Спасибо.**
[Spa-see-ba]

4 How much is it?

CUSTOMER **Сколько это стоит?**
[Skóly-ka é-ta stó-eet?]

TRADER **Пятьдесят три копейки[6].**
[Pee-dye-syát tree ka-pyéy-kee]

5 How much are they?

CUSTOMER **Сколько стоят?**
[Skóly-ka stó-yat?]

TRADER **Тридцать пять копеек.**
[Tree-tsaty pyaty ka-pyé-yek]

6 How much is one postcard?

CUSTOMER **А ско́лько сто́ит одна́[4] откры́тка[3]?**
[A skóly-ka stó-eet ad-ná at-krít-ka?]

KIOSK LADY **Шесть копе́ек.**
[Shesty ka-pyé-yek]

CUSTOMER **Спаси́бо большо́е.**
[Spa-sée-ba baly-shó-ye]

7 Buying two envelopes for England

CUSTOMER **Мне, пожа́луйста, два[5] конве́рта, самолётом.***
[Mnye, pa-zhál-sta, dva kan-vyér-ta, sa-ma-lyó-tam]

ASSISTANT **Оди́н рубль две[5] копе́йки, пожа́луйста. Оди́н рубль две копе́йки.**
[A-déen roobly, dvye ka-pyéy-kee]

CUSTOMER **Хорошо́.** [Ha-ra-shó]

* For me, please, two airmail envelopes. **Самолётом** means 'by plane'.

8 Buying two stamped postcards for England

CUSTOMER **Здра́вствуйте.**

ASSISTANT **Здра́вствуйте.**

CUSTOMER **Мне, пожа́луйста, две откры́тки.**
[Mnye, pa-zhál-sta, dvye at-krít-kee]

ASSISTANT **Две откры́тки – се́мьдесят копе́ек, пожа́луйста.** [Dvye at-krít-kee – syém-dye-syat ka-pyé-yek]

CUSTOMER **Ско́лько? Повтори́те ещё раз.***
[Skóly-ka? Pa-fta-rée-tye ye-shshyó ras]

ASSISTANT **Се́мьдесят. Се́мьдесят.**
[Syém-dye-syat]

CUSTOMER **Спаси́бо.**

ASSISTANT **Пожа́луйста. Пожа́луйста.**

* Repeat again.

9 Twenty envelopes and five postcards

ASSISTANT **Двадцать конвёртов[7] стоят рубль двадцать. И пять открыток[7] стоят тридцать копеек. Всего рубль пятьдесят.***
[Dvá-tsaty kan-vyér-taf stó-yat roobly dvá-tsaty. Ee pyaty at-krí-tak stó-yat treé-tsaty ka-pyé-yek. Fsye-vó roobly pee-dye-syát]

CUSTOMER **Простите, сколько?**
[Pra-steé-tye, skóly-ka?]

ASSISTANT **Рубль пятьдесят.**
[Roobly pee-dye-syát]

CUSTOMER **Спасибо.**

ASSISTANT **Пожалуйста. Пожалуйста.**

* Altogether (one) rouble fifty (kopecks).

10 Two stamped airmail envelopes

CUSTOMER **Здравствуйте, я хочу послать письмо в Англию.* Сколько это стоит?**
[Ya ha-choʼo pa-sláty peesy-mó v Án-glee-yoo. Skóly-ka é-ta stó-eet?]

ASSISTANT **Пятьдесят одна копейка.**
[Pee-dye-syát ad-ná ka-pyéy-ka]

CUSTOMER **Два конвёрта, пожалуйста.**
[Dva kan-vyér-ta, pa-zhál-sta]

ASSISTANT **Так, пожалуйста. Рубль две.**
[Tak, pa-zhál-sta. Roobly dvye]

* Hello, I want to send a letter to England.

11 Asking prices in the Beriozka

CUSTOMER **Сколько стоит водка?**
[Skóly-ka stó-eet vót-ka?]

ASSISTANT **Столичная водка пять рублей десять копеек. Пять десять.**
[Sta-leéch-na-ya vót-ka pyaty roo-blyéy dyé-syaty ka-pyé-yek. Pyaty dyé-syaty]

CUSTOMER **А сколько стоит Пепси-Кола?**
[A skóly-ka stó-eet Pép-see-Kó-la?]

ASSISTANT **Пе́пси-Ко́ла сто́ит со́рок пять копе́ек.**
[Pép-see-Kó-la stó-eet só-rak pyaty ka-pyé-yek]

12 An amenable market trader selling pears

CUSTOMER **Ско́лько сто́ят ва́ши гру́ши?**
[Skóly-ka stó-yat vá-shi groó-shi?]

TRADER **Пятна́дцать рубле́й.**
[Peet-ná-tsaty roo-blyéy]

CUSTOMER **А е́сли за де́сять рубле́й?***
[A yé-slee za dyé-syaty roo-blyéy?]

TRADER **Мо́жно****. Мо́жно, мо́жно, мо́жно.**
[Mózh-na]

* What if I offer ten?
** It's possible (=OK).

13 But this apple seller is less willing to bargain

CUSTOMER **Здра́вствуйте, ско́лько сто́ят ва́ши
я́блоки?** [Skóly-ka stó-yat vá-shi
yá-bla-kee?]

TRADER **Я́блоки сто́ят пять рубле́й килогра́мм.**
[Yá-bla-kee stó-yat pyaty roo-blyéy kee-la-grám]

CUSTOMER **Ой, э́то о́чень до́рого[8]. А за три
рубля́?** [Óy, é-ta ó-chyeny dó-ra-ga. A
za tree roo-blyá?]

TRADER **За три рубля́ нет.**
[Za tree roo-blyá nyet]

14 In many shops if you want to examine an item you must ask the assistant to show it to you

TOURIST **Покажи́те, пожа́луйста, во́т э́то.***
[Pa-ka-zhí-tye, pa-zhál-sta, vót é-ta]

ASSISTANT **Э́то?** [É-ta?]

TOURIST **Нет** [Nyet]

ASSISTANT **Э́то?**

TOURIST **Да.** [Da]

ASSISTANT **Пожа́луйста.**

* Please show me that over there.

Word List

The word lists in the units give the words you should try to learn. Other words which occur in the conversations are in the full Russian–English list at the end of the book.

m = masculine; f = feminine; n = neuter

а [a]	but/and (slight contrast)
ва́ши [vá-shi]	your
во́т [vót]	here is/there is
да [da]	yes
до́рого [dó-ra-ga]	expensive
е́сли [yé-slee]	if
за [za]	for
и [ee]	and
кило́ (n) [kee-ló]	kilo
килогра́мм (m) [kee-la-grám]	kilogram
конве́рт (m) [kan-vyért]	envelope
мне [mnye]	for me/to me
мо́жно [mózh-na]	it's possible
нет [nyet]	no
откры́тка (f) [at-krít-ka]	postcard
о́чень [ó-chyeny]	very
письмо́ (n) [peesy-mó]	letter
повтори́те [pa-fta-ree-tye]	repeat
скажи́те [ska-zhí-tye]	tell (me)
Столи́чная (f) [Sta-lée ch-na-ya]	Stolichnaya (brand of vodka)
так [tak]	so
э́то [é-ta]	this/that/it
я хочу́ [ya ha-choó]	I want

Explanations

1 Numbers 11-100

You already know the numbers from 1 to 10 (see page 22). The teens are formed by putting 1 to 9, sometimes with small spelling changes, in front of **на** [na] 'on' and **дцать** [tsaty], a form of **де́сять** 'ten':

11	**оди́ннадцать**	[a-dée-na-tsaty] = 'one on ten'
12	**двена́дцать**	[dvye-ná-tsaty] = 'two on ten'
13	**трина́дцать**	[tree-ná-tsaty]
14	**четы́рнадцать**	[chye-tír-na-tsaty]
15	**пятна́дцать**	[peet-ná-tsaty]
16	**шестна́дцать**	[shes-ná-tsaty]
17	**семна́дцать**	[syem-ná-tsaty]
18	**восемна́дцать**	[va-syem-ná-tsaty]
19	**девятна́дцать**	[dye-veet-ná-tsaty]

The numbers 20, 30, 50 and so on are made up in a similar way, but with no **на**; 40 and 90 are exceptions:

20	**два́дцать**	[dvá-tsaty] 'two ten'
30	**три́дцать**	[trée-tsaty] 'three ten'
40	**со́рок**	[só-rak]
50	**пятьдеся́т**	[pee-dye-syát] 'five ten'
60	**шестьдеся́т**	[shez-dye-syát]
70	**се́мьдесят**	[syém-dye-syat]
80	**во́семьдесят**	[vó-syem-dye-syat]
90	**девяно́сто**	[dye-vee-nó-sta]

100 **сто́** [stó]

Compound numbers (21, 49 etc.) are formed as in English:

21 = 20 (**два́дцать**) + 1 (**оди́н**) [dvá-tsaty a-deen]:
    два́дцать оди́н
42 **со́рок два** [só-rak dva]
137 **сто́ три́дцать семь** (NB no 'and')

2 It/this/that

Это [É-ta] is the word to use when you don't know what something is called. It means 'it', 'this' and also 'that'.

What does it/this/that cost? **Сколько это стоит?** [Skóly-ka é-ta stó-eet?]

3 Gender of nouns

Russian nouns (words for things like 'envelope', 'postcard', 'letter') are masculine (m), feminine (f) or neuter (n). Words that end with a consonant, e.g. **конверт** [kan-vyért] 'envelope', are masculine; if the last letter is -a, the word is feminine, e.g. **открытка** [at-krít-ka] 'postcard'; the small number of nouns ending in -o are neuter, e.g. **письмо** [peesy-mó] 'letter'. Nouns ending with other letters are less predictable; the gender is shown in the word list in each unit.

4 One

The word for 'one' is

один [a-déen] with masculine words
одна [ad-ná] with feminine ones
одно [ad-nó] with neuter ones

один конверт [a-déen kan-vyért] one envelope
одна открытка [ad-ná at-krít-ka] one postcard
одно письмо [ad-nó peesy-mó] one letter

The same forms are used with compound numbers ending 'one' (21, 31, etc), and the noun is always *singular*:

пятьдесят одна копейка fifty-one kopecks [pee-dye-syát ad-ná ka-pyéy-ka] (literally 'fifty-one kopeck')

двадцать один рубль twenty-one roubles (literally 'twenty-one rouble')

5 Two

Two is **два** [dva] with masculine and neuter nouns, **две** [dvye] with feminine ones.

Рубль [roobly], the Soviet unit of currency, is masculine:

Два рубля [dva roo-blyá] 'two roubles'

Копейка [ka-pyéy-ka], 'kopeck', one hundredth of a rouble, is feminine:
Две копейки [dvye ka-pyéy-kee] 'two kopecks'

The same applies to compound numbers ending in 'two' (22, 142 etc.)
Двадцать два рубля 'twenty-two roubles'
[Dvá-tsaty dva roo-blyá]

6 Two, three, four of something

You may have noticed that in the last example **рубль** [roobly] became **рубля** [roo-blyá] and **копейка** became **копейки** [ka-pyéy-kee]. This is because Russian is an inflected language, which means the endings of words change depending on the grammar of the sentence.

After the numbers two, three and four, nouns have an ending (called the genitive singular) which means 'of':
'Two/three/four roubles' is **два/три/четыре рубля** [dva/tree/chye-tí-rye roo-blyá], meaning literally 'two/three/four of rouble'.
'Three kopecks' is **три копейки** [tree ka-pyéy-kee], which means 'three of kopeck'.

You find the same forms after 22, 23, 24 and all higher numbers ending 2, 3, 4:
сорок два рубля 42 roubles [só-rak dva roo-blyá]

7 Five, six, seven...

After five and larger numbers, Russian uses another ending. **Рубль** becomes **рублей** [roo-blyéy], which means 'of roubles', and **копейка** becomes **копеек** [ka-pyé-yek] 'of kopecks'. This ending is called the genitive plural.

Here are some more examples of things you may want to count:
одна открытка   [ad-ná at-krít-ka]   1 postcard
три открытки   [tree at-krít-kee]   3 postcards

пять откры́ток   [pyaty at-krí-tak]   5 postcards

оди́н конве́рт   [a-de'en kan-vyért]   1 envelope
два конве́рта   [dva kan-vyér-ta]   2 envelopes
шесть конве́ртов   [shesty kan-vyér-taf]
   6 envelopes

Don't worry about the details of all these endings at this stage. Learning Russian grammar is a big job, but, fortunately, you don't need much to 'get by'. In this book we'll try not to overburden you.

8   That is very expensive

Э́то о́чень до́рого   [É-ta ó-chyeny dó-ra-ga]
'That very expensive'. Russian does not require any equivalent of 'is', 'am', 'are'.

Exercises

1   What is the price?   (You'll hear the word **чесно́к** [chyes-nók], which means garlic.)

CUSTOMER   Ско́лько сто́ит чесно́к?
TRADER   Пять рубле́й. Пять рубле́й.
CUSTOMER   Спаси́бо.

2   How much must the customer pay?

ASSISTANT   Э́то сто́ит со́рок копе́ек.
CUSTOMER   Со́рок копе́ек? Пожа́луйста.

3   In the shop

(a) Ask how much it costs.
(b) Ask the assistant to give you three.
(c) Tell the cashier that you have to pay two roubles ten kopecks.

4   Play the part of the customer

CUSTOMER   (Ask how much a postcard costs)
ASSISTANT   Шесть копе́ек.
CUSTOMER   (Ask for two)
ASSISTANT   Пожа́луйста, двена́дцать копе́ек.
CUSTOMER   (Say thank you)
ASSISTANT   Пожа́луйста.

5 Play the part of the customer

CUSTOMER	(Ask the price of the apples)
TRADER	Пятна́дцать рубле́й килогра́мм.
CUSTOMER	(Offer eight)
TRADER	Нет. Двена́дцать.
CUSTOMER	(Offer ten)
TRADER	Оди́ннадцать.
CUSTOMER	(Accept eleven)
TRADER	Хорошо́. Ско́лько кило́?
CUSTOMER	(Say one kilogramme)

6 How much do you owe?

Со́рок четы́ре копе́йки.

7 How much do you owe?

Шестьдеся́т шесть копе́ек. Шестьдеся́т шесть.

8 What do the signs say?

(a)

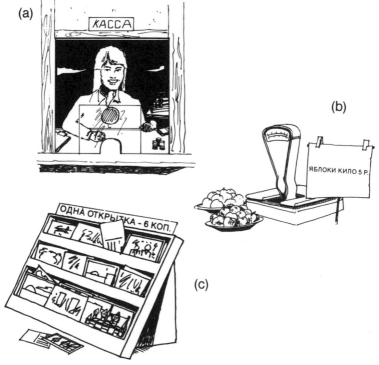

КАССА

(b)

ЯБЛОКИ КИЛО 5 Р.

ОДНА ОТКРЫТКА – 6 КОП.

(c)

Worth knowing

Shopping in the USSR

Shopping is not likely to be the highlight of your Soviet trip. Russian shops generally strike Westerners as empty. So be sure to take with you everything you can't do without: toiletries, medicines, soap, instant coffee, toothpaste, all clothes, a bath plug. In the Soviet Union you are unlikely to be able to replace things you forgot to pack. Imported consumer goods are rare, and Russians freely admit that the quality of their own products lags well behind the West. A consignment of good-quality goods lies on the counter for as long as it takes the long snaking queue to buy the whole lot. So do *not* expect to spend much time or money in ordinary Soviet shops.

The USSR has food supermarkets where you can simply take things off the shelves and pay for them at the check-out without saying a word. In a few shops you can simply point at what you want and pay the assistant. But in most shops (including the foreign currency Beriozkas), before you receive goods you must pay for them at a cash desk some distance from the counter where they are sold. This means you may have to list your intended purchases and their prices to the cashier without being able to point at them. You decide what you want to buy, note the price, queue at the cash desk (**кácca** [ká-ssa]), tell the cashier what you want and he, or, usually, she, gives you a receipt (**чек** [chyek]) for each purchase. You take these **чéки** to the relevant counters and hand them over for the goods.

In state shops prices are fixed and the price is marked (often printed) on nearly everything. There is no need to 'shop around' because the state price is the same everywhere. But many things, such as good-quality fruit, are often only available in the private or farm markets (**рынок** [rí-nak] 'market') at prices higher than the state ones, and you may have to ask what the prices are. Sometimes there is room for bargaining.

The Beriozka shops

To earn foreign currency and to make things easier for foreigners, there are special shops called 'Beriozka' (**Берёзка** means 'little birch tree'). These shops, which usually have blank windows to conceal the goods inside from envious Soviet citizens, stock scarce or imported goods and sell them only for convertible currencies such as pounds, dollars and German marks. They usually have books and records, vodka, wine, coffee, souvenirs, and sometimes fur hats, caviare, electrical goods and some of the everyday items which happen to be in short supply (perhaps toilet paper, razor blades, toothpaste). Every Intourist hotel has a Beriozka.

Soviet money

The Soviet unit of currency is the rouble, which comes in paper denominations of one, three, five, ten, twenty-five, fifty and a hundred. Try to avoid notes above ten – and if you do take the risk of changing money on the black market (illegal, but very tempting, since you will be offered anything up to fifteen times the offical rate!) don't take hundred-rouble notes and beware of fakes. The rouble is divided into one hundred kopecks, which come in coins of 1, 2, 3, 5, 10, 15, 20 and 50. One-rouble coins are also quite common and they make good souvenirs. Although the import and export of Soviet currency is illegal, customs officers don't object if you take coins with you.

3 Food and Drink

Key expressions

Is there	**Есть?** [Yesty?]
Is there coffee?	**Есть кофе?** [Yesty kó-fye?]
Have you got...?	**У вас есть...?** [Oo vas yesty...?]
Have you any beer?	**У вас есть пиво?** [Oo vas yesty pée-va?]
What have you got?	**Что у вас есть?** [Shtó oo vas yesty?]
There isn't any Pepsi	**Пепси нет** [Pép-see nyet]
Big	**Большой** [Baly-shóy]
Small	**Маленький** [Má-lyeny-kee]
With sugar	**С сахаром** [Ssá-ha-ram]
Without sugar	**Без сахара** [Byes sá-ha-ra]
A cheese sandwich	**Бутерброд с сыром** [Boo-tyer-brót ssi-ram]
A bottle of mineral water, please	**Бутылку минеральной воды, пожалуйста** [Boo-tíl-koo mee-nye-rály-nay va-dí, pa-zhál-sta]
The bill, please	**Счёт, пожалуйста** [Shshyot, pa-zhál-sta]

Conversations

1   Have you any coffee?

MAN   **У вас есть[1,2] кóфе?**
[Oo vas yesty kó-fye?]

SNACKBAR GIRL   **Да, есть.[3]**
[Da, yesty]

MAN   **Два кóфе[4], пожáлуйста.**
[Dva kó-fye, pa-zhál-sta]

2   Big or small, with or without sugar?

GIRL   **Вам большóй úли мáленький?**
[Vam baly-shóy ée-lee má-lyeny-kee?]

MAN   **Большóй.**

GIRL   **С сáхаром[6]?**
[Ssá-ha-ram?]

MAN   **Да, с сáхаром, пожáлуйста.**

3   Open sandwiches and a drink.

GIRL   **Я вас слýшаю.**

CUSTOMER   **У вас есть бутербрóды?***
[Oo vas yesty boo-tyer-bró-di?]

GIRL   **С колбасóй[6] и с сýром.**
[Skal-ba-sóy ee ssír-am]

CUSTOMER   **Я не знáю[7]. С колбасóй – два. И два с сýром.**
[Ya nye zná-yoo. Skal-ba-sóy – dva. Ee dva ssí-ram]

GIRL   **Пожáлуйста. А чтó вы бýдете пить?****
[A shtó vi bóo-dye-tye peety?]

CUSTOMER   **Пéпси, пожáлуйста.**

GIRL   **Пéпси нет[5].**
[Pép-see nyet]

CUSTOMER   **Тогдá пúво.**
[Tag-dá pée-va]

GIRL   **Пúва тóже нет[5].**
[Pée-va tó-zhe nyet]

CUSTOMER   **А чтó есть?**
[A shtó yesty?]

GIRL   **Со́к и минера́льная вода́.**
[Sók ee mee-nye-rály-na-ya va-dá]

CUSTOMER   **Буты́лку[8] минера́льной воды́[9], пожа́луйста.**
[Boo-tíl-koo mee-nye-rály-nay va-dí, pa-zhál-sta]

*Have you (any) sandwiches?
**And what will you drink?

4   What *have* you got to drink?

CUSTOMER   **Пи́во, пожалуйста.**
[Pée-va, pa-zhál-sta]

GIRL   **Пи́ва не́ту.**
[Pée-va nyé-too]

CUSTOMER   **Вино́ есть?**
[Vee-nó yesty?]

GIRL   **Нет.**

CUSTOMER   **А во́дка есть?**
[A vót-ka yesty?]

GIRL   **То́же нет.**
[Tó-zhe nyet]

CUSTOMER   **А что́ же у вас есть?***
[A shtó zhe oo vas yesty?]

GIRL   **Есть со́к и Пе́пси. Минера́льная вода́.**
[Yesty sók ee Pép-see. Mee-nye-rály-na-ya va-dá]

CUSTOMER   **Како́й со́к?**
[Ka-kóy sók?]

GIRL   **Апельси́новый.**
[A-pyely-seé-na-vi]

CUSTOMER   **Оди́н, пожа́луйста.**

GIRL   **Пожа́луйста.**

*What *have* you got then? **же** [zhe] makes the question emphatic.

5   Ordering borshsh, a hamburger and ice cream

WAITER   **До́брый ве́чер. Во́т вам меню́, пожа́луйста.**
[Dó-bri vyé-chyer. Vót vam mye-nyoó]

DINER **Добрый вечер. Борщ, пожалуйста, и на второе блюдо бифштекс. ***
[Borshsh, pa-zhál-sta, ee na fta-ró-ye blyoó-da beef-shtéks]

WAITER **Что вы будете на десерт?****
[Shtó vi boó-dye-tye na dye-syért?]

DINER **На десерт мороженое.**
[Na dye-syért ma-ró-zhe-na-ye]

WAITER **Одну минуту. ***** *Had on a*
[Ad-noó mee-noó-too] *a meenit Scots*

* and for the main course a hamburger.

** What will you have for dessert?

*** Just a minute

6 Some wine

DINER **А что у вас есть выпить?**
[A shtó oo vas yesty ví-peety?]

WAITRESS **Есть вино сухое. Белое, красное. Какое вы будете?***
[Yesty vee-nó soo-hó-ye. Byé-la-ye, krá-sna-ye. Ka-kó-ye vi boó-dye-tye?]

DINER **Пожалуйста, белое вино.**
[... byé-la-ye vee-nó]

WAITRESS **Пожалуйста.**

* What kind will you take?

be so kind

7 A vegetarian

DINER **Официант, будьте добры. ***
[A-fee-tsi-ánt, boó-tye da-brí]

WAITRESS **Пожалуйста, я вас слушаю.**

DINER **Я вегетарианец.**
[Ya vye-gye-ta-ree-á-nyets]

WAITRESS **Вы будете есть рыбу? ****
[Vi boó-dye-tye yesty rí-boo?]

DINER **Нет, я ем только овощи. *****
[Nyet, ya yem tóly-ka ó-va-shshee]

WAITRESS **Хорошо, я принесу для вас овощи.******
[Ha-ra-shó, ya pree-nye-soó dlya vas ó-va-shshee]

| DINER | Спаси́бо. |
| WAITRESS | Пожа́луйста. |

* Waiter, excuse me (lit. 'be so good')
** Will you eat fish?
*** I eat only vegetables.
**** All right, I'll bring you (for you) vegetables.

То́лько / only
=

8 The bill, please

DINER	Официа́нт. Счёт, пожа́луйста.
	[A-fee-tsi-ánt. Shshyot]
WAITRESS	Пожа́луйста, с вас* четы́ре рубля́ девяно́сто пять копе́ек.
	[svas chye-tí-rye roo-blyá dye-vee-nó-sta pyaty ka-pyé-yek]
DINER	Ско́лько, прости́те?
	[Skóly-ka, pra-stée-tye?]
WAITRESS	Четы́ре рубля́ девяно́сто пять копе́ек.

* You owe (lit. 'from you').

Word list

апельси́новый сок (m) [a-pyely-sée-na-vi sók]	orange juice
без [byes]	without
бе́лое вино́ (n) [byé-la-ye vee-nó]	white wine
бифште́кс (m) [beef-shtéks]	'beefsteak', meat rissole, hamburger
большо́й [baly-shóy]	large
борщ (m) [bórshsh]	beetroot soup
бутербро́д (m) [boo-tyer-brót]	open sandwich
буты́лка (f) [boo-tíl-ka]	bottle
вам [vam]	to you/for you
вино́ (n) [vee-nó]	wine
вода́ (f) [va-dá]	water
во́дка (f) [vót-ka]	vodka
вот [vót]	here (pointing)
второ́е блю́до (n) [fta-ró-ye blyóo-da]	second course (main course)

на второе [na fta-ró-ye]	for the main course
выпить [ví-peety]	to drink (alcohol)
десéрт (m) [dye-syért]	dessert
на десéрт [na dye-syért]	for dessert
для [dlya]	for (somebody)
для вас [dlya vas]	for you
(я) ем [(ya) yem]	(I) eat
есть [yesty]	is/are
есть [yesty]	to eat
я знáю [ya zná-yoo]	I know
я не знáю [ya nye zná-yoo]	I don't know
или [ée-lee]	or
какóй [ka-kóy]	what kind of
колбасá (f) [kal-ba-sá]	salami
с колбасóй [skal-ba-sóy]	with salami
крáсное винó (n) [krá-sna-ye vee-nó]	red wine
мáленький [má-lyeny-kee]	small
меню́ (n) [mye-nyóo]	menu
минерáльная водá (f) [mee-nye-rály-na-ya]	mineral water
морóженое (n) [ma-ró-zhe-na-ye]	ice cream
нет [nyet]	there is no
нéту [nyé-too] (coll.)	there is no
óвощи (m) [ó-va-shshee]	vegetables
официáнт (m) [a-fee-tsi-ánt]	waiter/waitress
пиво (n) [pée-va]	beer
пить [peety]	to drink
рыба (f) [rí-ba]	fish
с [s]	with
с вас [svas]	from you
сáхар (m) [sá-har]	sugar
сóк (m) [sók]	juice
сухóе винó (n) [soo-hó-ye vee-nó]	dry wine
счёт (m) [shshyot]	bill

сыр (m) [sir]   cheese
   с сы́ром [ssí-ram]   with cheese
тогда́ [tag-dá]   then
то́же [tó-zhe]   too
то́лько [tóly-ka]   only
у вас [oo vas]   you have
что́ [shtó]   what
что́ же [shtó zhe]   what (more emphatic)

Explanations

1 Is there...?/Are there...?

Есть [yesty] 'is'/'are' is used when you want to know if something is available:

Is there tea?	**Есть чай?**
Are there sandwiches?	**Есть бутербро́ды?**
Is there wine?	**Есть вино́?**
Is there any beer?	**Есть пи́во?**

The order of words is flexible. You can also say **Чай есть?**, **Вино́ есть?** etc.

If you have the cassette, listen to the voice rising on **есть** in these questions.

2 Have you got?

The same useful word **есть** occurs in the Russian construction for 'have':

У вас есть ко́фе?   Have you any coffee?
[Oo vas yesty kó-fye?]
This means literally 'By (**у**) you (**вас**) is (**есть**) coffee (**ко́фе**)?

Have you any sandwiches?	**У вас есть бутербро́ды?**

3 There is/there are

If something is available, you hear the same word, **есть**.

Да, есть	Yes, there is
Есть со́к и Пе́пси	There is juice and Pepsi

Виио́ есть?   Is there any wine?
Виио́ есть.   There is wine.

Notice that in spoken Russian, the difference between these two sentences is the voice rising on **есть** in the question.

4   Coffee and Pepsi: easy words

'Coffee', which we met in unit 1, is **ко́фе** [kó-fye], a masculine noun. 'Two coffees', or, as the Russians say, 'two of coffee', is **два ко́фе** [dva kó-fye]. You see that there is no change in the form of the word **ко́фе**. In fact, **ко́фе** never changes its form, regardless of grammar. Because of its foreign origin and (to a Russian) foreign sound, it doesn't obey the usual grammatical rules. The same is true of the foreign word **Пе́пси** [Pép-see].

5   There isn't any/aren't any

Нет (the same as the word for 'no') means 'there isn't' or 'there aren't'. There is also a colloquial form **не́ту** [nyé-too].

Ко́фе нет (or **Нет ко́фе**) means 'There's no coffee'
Пе́пси нет [Pép-see nyet] 'There's no Pepsi'
Пи́ва не́ту [Pée-va nyé-too] 'There's no beer'
Во́дки нет [Vót-kee nyet] 'There's no vodka'

You may have noticed the change in the ending of **пи́во** 'beer' and **во́дка** 'vodka' with **нет**. **Пи́ва** means 'of beer' and **во́дки** means 'of vodka'. In Russian, when **нет** means 'there isn't/aren't', nouns are put in a form called the *genitive*, which means 'of'. So **Во́дки нет** literally means 'There isn't of vodka'. **Ко́фе** and **Пе́пси** don't change their endings, as explained in 4 above.

6   With

After the short word **с** meaning 'with', Russian words add endings called the *instrumental case* (just a grammatical name). Here are some examples:

сáхар 'sugar';   **с сáхаром** 'with sugar'
сыр 'cheese';   **с сыром** with cheese'
колбасá 'salami';   **с колбасóй** 'with sausage'

7   I know/I don't know

Я знáю [Ya zná-yoo] is 'I know'. To make it negative, simply put **не** in front of **знáю**: **Я не знáю** [Ya nye zná-yoo] 'I don't know'.

8   (Bring me) a bottle

Бутылку [boo-tíl-koo] is a form of the word **бутылка** [boo-tíl-ka] 'bottle'. The ending of **бутылку** is called the *accusative case* and is used to show the object of a verb, as opposed to the subject. The customer's phrase is short for *'Bring me* a bottle'. 'Bottle' is the object of the verb 'to bring' and so the accusative ending is used, just as in English we say, 'Bring her', not 'Bring she'. Russian nouns ending in -**a** all change the -**a** to -**y** in the accusative. Most other nouns don't change.

9   A bottle of mineral water

The 'of' in 'of something' corresponds to the Russian genitive case endings, the endings we met after **нет** 'there isn't' in 5 above. **Минерáльная водá** 'mineral water' becomes **минерáльной воды** [mee-nye-rály-nay va-dí] if you want to say 'of mineral water'.

Exercises

1   Read the following list of drinks, then listen to the real-life café dialogue and mark which of the drinks are available. There are some words you haven't met yet (they are in the key) but you should concentrate on recognising the words you've learnt so far.

минерáльная водá	mineral water
вóдка	vodka

ко́фе без молока́	coffee without milk/black coffee
ко́фе с молоко́м	coffee with milk/white coffee
Пе́пси-Ко́ла	Pepsi-Cola
лимона́д [lee-ma-nát]	lemonade

A Скажи́те, пожа́луйста, у вас есть минера́льная вода́?
B Нет, минера́льной воды́ сего́дня нет.
A А скажи́те, пожа́луйста, у вас есть во́дка?
B Нет, у нас во́дки не быва́ет.
A Спаси́бо. А у вас есть сего́дня ко́фе?
B Да, ко́фе есть. То́лько без молока́.
A А есть Пе́пси-Ко́ла и́ли лимона́д?
B Есть лимона́д. Пе́пси-Ко́лы нет.
A Спаси́бо.

2 What does the customer decide to order?

CUSTOMER Я возьму́ ча́шку ко́фе.
WAITER Большо́й и́ли ма́ленький?
CUSTOMER Ма́ленький.
WAITER С са́харом?
CUSTOMER Да.
WAITER Два́дцать шесть копе́ек, пожа́луйста.

3 How much do you owe?

WAITER Вот вам счёт, пожа́луйста. С вас де́сять рубле́й со́рок копе́ек.

4 You are the customer

YOU (Waiter, the bill, please)
WAITER С вас де́вять рубле́й во́семь копе́ек.
YOU (Ask him to repeat)
WAITER Де́вять рубле́й во́семь копе́ек.

5 How much do you owe?

(a) С вас во́семь рубле́й три́дцать копе́ек.
(b) С вас пятьдеся́т копе́ек.
(c) С вас три рубля́ пятна́дцать копе́ек.
(d) С вас двена́дцать рубле́й во́семьдесят шесть копе́ек.

6 Play the part of the customer

YOU   (Excuse me, is there any coffee?)
WAITER   Ко́фе нет.
YOU   (Is there any vodka?)
WAITER   Во́дки то́же нет.
YOU   (Is there any tea?)
WAITER   Ча́я то́же нет.
YOU   (What have you got?)
WAITER   Есть Пе́пси, минера́льная вода́, лимона́д.
YOU   (Mineral water, please)
WAITER   Ско́лько буты́лок?*
YOU   (Two, please)
WAITER   Пожа́луйста, с вас се́мьдесят копе́ек.

* 'How many (of) bottles?'

Worth knowing

Soviet restaurants

A Soviet package tour includes all meals, and no choice of menu will be offered. The fare will be standard international, with a lot of chicken and beef. Bread, white and black, is served at all meals; breakfast may include one of the yogurt-type drinks such as **кефи́р** [kye-fe'er] or **простоква́ша** [pra-sta-kvá-sha]; lunch always includes soup. Mineral water (**минера́льная вода́**), tea (**чай**) and coffee (**ко́фе**), and sometimes beer (**пи́во**) will be brought automatically. The only Russian you will need is for special requests, such as vegetarian food. But be warned that Russians associate meat with the good life and find vegetarianism almost incomprehensible. Although hotel restaurants are getting used to foreign vegetarians and understand the implications of **Я вегетариа́нец** [Ya vye-gye-ta-ree-án-ets] (if you're a man) or **Я вегетариа́нка** [Ya vye-gye-ta-ree-án-ka] (if you're a woman), they will often just bring an omelette or the meat dish minus the meat (i.e. just the vegetables). There is little point in making a fuss about the dullness of this diet: vegetarian cooking is *not* part of Russian culture.

For real Russian cooking, you will have to get yourself invited to Russian homes (see Unit 6). To try non-Russian cooking, there are ethnic restaurants in Moscow, such as the Georgian **Арáгви** [A-rág-vee], the Uzbek **Узбекистáн** [Ooz-

МЕНЮ

АРАГВИ

bye-kee-stán] or the Armenian **Армéния** [Ar-myé-nee-ya]. To avoid lengthy queuing in the street, get your hotel Service Bureau to book you a table. The extensive menu will be in several languages, including English, but only those items which have prices are available. Your need for Russian will be minimal.

The recent appearance of 'cooperative' (private) restaurants means that the gastronomic scene is changing – and improving. So if you want a change from the unadventurous food of the state hotels and restaurants, get a Russian friend to take you to a cooperative (**кооперати́в** [ka-a-pye-ra-te'ef]). You pay the not inconsiderable bill, your friend will do the explaining and interpreting.

4 Getting around town

Key expressions

Tell me please	**Скажи́те, пожа́луйста** [Ska-zhí-tye]
Where is ...?	**Где ...?** [Gdye...?]
Red Square	**Кра́сная пло́щадь** [Krá-sna-ya pló-shshyaty]
On/to the left	**Нале́во** [Na-lyé-va]
On/to the right	**Напра́во** [Na-prá-va]
Straight on	**Пря́мо** [Pryá-ma]
Far	**Далеко́** [Da-lye-kó]
Not far	**Недалеко́** [Nye-da-lye-kó]
Round the corner	**За угло́м** [Za oo-glóm]
Along the street	**По у́лице** [Pa óo-lee-tse]
How do I get to the Russian Museum (on foot)?	**Как пройти́ в Ру́сский музе́й?** [Kak pray-tée v Róo-skee moo-zyéy?]
When do I get off?	**Когда́ выходи́ть?** [Kag-dá vi-ha-déety?]
Are you getting off?	**Вы выхо́дите?** [Vi vi-hó-dee-tye?]
The next stop	**Сле́дующая остано́вка** [Slyé-doo-yoo-shshya-ya a-sta-nóf-ka]
At the next stop	**На сле́дующей остано́вке**
Pass (my ticket) along, please	**Переда́йте, пожа́луйста** [Pye-rye-dáy-tye]
I don't understand	**Я не понима́ю** [Ya nye pa-nee-má-yoo]

Conversations

1 Finding Gorky Street (Moscow's main street)

VISITOR	**Пожа́луйста, скажи́те[1], где[2] у́лица Го́рького?**
	[Pa-zhál-sta, ska-zhí-tye, gdye oó-lee-tsa Góry-ka-va?]
PASSER-BY	**Пря́мо и напра́во.**
	[Pryá-ma ee na-prá-va]

2 Where's Red Square, please?

TOURIST	**Скажи́те, пожа́луйста, где Кра́сная пло́щадь?**
	[Ska-zhí-tye, pa-zhál-sta, gdye Krá-sna-ya pló-shshyaty?]
MUSCOVITE	**За угло́м и по у́лице, пря́мо.**
	[Za oo-glóm ee pa oó-lee-tse, pryá-ma]

3 Where's the post office, please?

VISITOR	**Прости́те, пожа́луйста, вы не зна́ете, где здесь по́чта?***
	[Pra-steé-tye, pa-zhál-sta, vi nye zná-ye-tye, gdye zdyesy póch-ta?]
PASSER-BY	**Зна́ю. Ря́дом. До́м шестьдеся́т два.****
	[Zná-yoo. Ryá-dam. Dóm shez-dye-syát dva]
VISITOR	**А где э́то?**
	[A gdye é-ta?]
PASSER-BY	**Во́т напра́во.*****
	[Vót na-prá-va]
VISITOR	**Спаси́бо большо́е.**
PASSER-BY	**Пожа́луйста. Пожа́луйста.**

* Do you know (= Don't you know) where the post office is here?
**I know. (It's) nearby. House (building) no. 62
***Over there on the right.

4 How do I get to the Russian Museum?

(The main museum in Leningrad for paintings by Russian artists)

| WOMAN | **Скажи́те, пожа́луйста, как пройти́ в[4] Ру́сский музе́й?** |
| | [Ska-zhí-tye, pa-zhál-sta, kak pray-teé v Roó-skee moo-zyéy?] |

MAN	**Пря́мо и нале́во.**
	[Pryá-ma ee na-lyé-va]
WOMAN	**Спаси́бо.**
MAN	**Пожа́луйста.**

5 How do I get there?

VISITOR	**Как прое́хать туда́[3]?**
	[Kak pra-yé-haty too-dá?]
MUSCOVITE	**На́до сесть на авто́бус и прое́хать три остано́вки.***
	[Ná-da syesty na af-tó-boos ee pra-yé-haty tree a-sta-nóf-kee]
VISITOR	**Спаси́бо.**
MUSCOVITE	**Пожа́луйста.**
VISITOR	**До свида́ния.**

*You have to take a bus and travel three stops.

6 How do I get to the Hermitage?
(Leningrad's most famous museum)

MAN	**До́брый день. Скажи́те, пожа́луйста, где Эрмита́ж?**
	[Dó-bri dyeny. Ska-zhí-tye, pa-zhál-sta, gdye Er-mee-tásh?]
WOMAN	**До́брый день. Он недалеко́ отсю́да*.**
	[Dó-bri dyeny. Ón nye-da-lye-kó at-syó-da]
MAN	**А как до него́ добра́ться?****
	[A kak da-nye-vó da-brá-tsa?]
WOMAN	**Вам лу́чше сесть на тролле́йбус но́мер оди́н.*****
	[Vam loó-che syesty na tra-lyéy-boos nó-myer a-deén]
MAN	**Большо́е спаси́бо.**
WOMAN	**Пожа́луйста.**

*He (= It) is not far from here.
**And how do I get to it?
***It would be best to take trolleybus no. 1.

7 You can't reach the ticket punch

PASSENGER 1	**Переда́йте, пожа́луйста, тало́н.**
	[Pye-rye-dáy-tye, pa-zhál-sta, ta-lón]
PASSENGER 2	**Хорошо́.** [Ha-ra-shó]

8 The Hermitage is the next stop

VISITOR **Эрмита́ж – когда́ выходи́ть?**
[Er-mee-tásh – kag-dá vi-ha-deéty?]

PASSENGER **На сле́дующей.***
[Na slyé-doo-yoo-shshyey]

VISITOR **Спаси́бо.**

PASSENGER **Не́ за что́.****
[Nyé za shtó]

*At the next (stop).
**You're welcome (= пожа́луйста).

9 Are you getting off?

PASSENGER 1 **Извини́те*, вы выхо́дите на
сле́дующей остано́вке[5]?**
[Eez-vee-neé-tye, vi vi-hó-dee-tye na
slyé-doo-yoo-shshyey a-sta-nóf-kye?]

PASSENGER 2 **Нет.**

*Excuse me (= Прости́те)

10 Are you getting off?

WOMAN **Вы выхо́дите на сле́дующей остано́вке?**

MAN **Да, выхожу́.**
[Da, vi-ha-zhoó]

DRIVER (announcing the next stop) **Садо́вая
у́лица* - сле́дующая остано́вка.**
[Sa-dó-va-ya oó-lee-tsa – slyé-doo-yoo-
shsha-ya a-sta-nóf-ka]

*Sadovaya Street crosses Nevsky Prospekt, Leningrad's main
avenue.

11 A friendly taxi driver

PASSENGER **Здра́вствуйте.**

TAXI DRIVER **Здра́вствуйте.**

PASSENGER **Мне на́до в Ки́ровский теа́тр.***
[Mnye ná-da fKeé-raf-skee tye-átr]

TAXI DRIVER **Пожа́луйста, сади́тесь.****
[Pa-zhál-sta, sa-deé-tyesy]

PASSENGER **Спаси́бо.**

*I have to go to the Kirov Theatre (Leningrad's equivalent of
Moscow's Bolshoi Theatre).

**Fine, get in.

Word list

авто́бус (m) [af-tó-boos]   bus
в [v] or [f]   in/to
выходи́ть [vi-ha-dée-ty]   to get out
  (я) выхожу́ [vi-ha-zhóo]   (I) am getting out
до [da]   as far as/until
добра́ться [da-brá-tsa]   to reach/get to
здесь [zdyesy]   here
как [kak]   how
когда́ [kag-dá]   when
лу́чше [lóo-che]   better
метро́ (n) [mye-tró]   metro/underground
мне на́до [mnye ná-da]   I have to
музе́й (m) [moo-zyéy]   museum
на [na]   on/to
на́до [ná-da]   it is necessary/one must
но́мер (m) [nó-myer]   number
о́н [ón]   he/it (if noun is masculine)
остано́вка (f)   stop
  [a-sta-nóf-ka]
отсю́да [at-syóo-da]   from here
пло́щадь (f)   square
  [pló-shshyaty]
переда́йте   pass (it) along
  [pye-rye-dáy-tye]
проспе́кт (m)   avenue
  [pra-spyékt]
сади́тесь   get in/sit down
  [sa-dée-tyesy]
сесть [syesty]   to get on (a bus etc.)/to sit down
такси́ (n) [tak-sée]   taxi
тало́н (m) [ta-lón]   travel coupon/ticket
теа́тр (m) [tye-átr]   theatre
трамва́й (m) [tram-váy]   tram
тролле́йбус (m)   trolleybus
  [tra-lyéy-boos]
у́лица (f) [óo-lee-tsa]   street
Эрмита́ж (m)   the Hermitage
  [Er-mee-tásh]

Explanations

1 Excuse me, can you tell me...?

Begin your request for information with **Прости́те, пожа́луйста** ('Excuse me please') or **Скажи́те, пожа́луйста** ('Tell me please').

Скажи́те, пожа́луйста, где метро́? Could you tell me where the metro is, please?

2 Asking where something is

The key word is **где** [gdye] 'where'. If you find [gdye] hard to say, miss out the [g] and say [dye]. Then add the name of the place.

Где Кра́сная пло́щадь? Where is Red Square?
[Gdye Krá-sna-ya pló-shshyaty?]
Remember there is no equivalent of 'is' in Russian.

Где метро́? Where is the metro?
Где музе́й? Where is the museum?

3 How do I get there?

'How' is **как** [kak]. If you want to walk, you ask **Как пройти́...?** (literally 'How to walk through...?'). If you want to use transport, you ask **Как прое́хать...?** (How to travel through...?). 'There' (in the sense of 'to that place') is **туда́** [too-dá].

Эрмита́ж, пожа́луйста. Как прое́хать туда́? The Hermitage, please. How do I get there (by transport)?

4 (How do I get) to the Russian Museum?

'To' is **в** ('into') with buildings, **на** ('onto') with streets and squares.

Как пройти́ в Ру́сский музе́й? How do I get (on foot) to the Russian Museum?
Как прое́хать в Эрмита́ж? How do I get (by transport) to the Hermitage?

After **в** 'into' and **на** 'onto', masculine and neuter words keep the same form as in the wordlists.

However, feminine nouns ending in -a (e.g. у́лица 'street') change their ending to -у (у́лицу). The ending -у is the accusative case, an ending we met in Unit 3.

Как прое́хать на у́лицу Го́рького? How do I get (by transport) to Gorky Street?
Как пройти́ в рестора́н Ара́гви? How do I get (on foot) to the Aragvi Restaurant?

5 Are you getting off?

You need the question **Вы выхо́дите?** [Vi vi-hó-dee-tye?] when you want to get off a bus or tram. Public transport is often very crowded. You push your way on at the back (look for **вход** [fhot] 'entrance'). To get to the exit doors (**вы́ход** [ví-hat] 'exit'), which are at the front, you may have to squeeze past a lot of large Russians. To give yourself enough time, start making for the exit well in advance. But instead of just pushing, ask the person blocking your path **Вы выхо́дите** [Vi vi-hó-dee-tye?] If the answer is **нет** [nyet], he/she will try to get out of your way. If it's **да** [da], just follow along behind while he/she does the asking.

Exercises

1 Give English equivalents for
(a) напра́во
(b) нале́во
(c) пря́мо
(d) На́до прое́хать три остано́вки.

2 Play the part of the visitor
VISITOR (Excuse me, where is the metro?)
RUSSIAN На́до сесть на тролле́йбус но́мер шесть и прое́хать две остано́вки.
VISITOR (Where is the stop?)
RUSSIAN Вот напра́во.
VISITOR (Thank you)
RUSSIAN Пожа́луйста.

3 Ask:

(a) where the Russia Hotel (гости́ница Росси́я) is.

(b) where the metro is.

(c) how to get to the Bolshoi Theatre (Большо́й теа́тр) on foot.

(d) how to get there by transport.

4 Fill in your part of the conversation and translate the answer

YOU   (Could you tell me where Red Square is, please?)

RUSSIAN   Кра́сная пло́щадь за угло́м и пря́мо по у́лице.

5 RUSSIAN   Вы выхо́дите?

YOU   (No)

What should you now do?

6 Fill in your part of the conversation (You won't recognise all the grammatical endings, but try to understand the meaning.)

YOU   (Excuse me, where is the Hermitage?)

RUSSIAN   Это далеко́. В нача́ле Не́вского проспе́кта.

YOU   (Excuse me, I don't understand. Please would you repeat?)

RUSSIAN   На Не́вском проспе́кте. Не́вский проспе́кт.

YOU   (And how do I get there by transport?)

RUSSIAN   Вам лу́чше сесть на тролле́йбус но́мер два́дцать два.

YOU   (Repeat, please)

RUSSIAN   Тролле́йбус но́мер два́дцать два.

YOU   (Thank you)

Worth knowing

Public transport

Many Soviet cities, including Moscow, Leningrad and Kiev, have a metro **(метро́)** 'underground', and all you need to travel any distance is a five-kopeck coin. There are no tickets. Simply put the coin in the slot beside the automatic barrier, watch for the white light, and pass through the narrow gap. If you don't put in a coin, two metal arms shoot out of the barrier with a crash and attempt to chop you in half.

Moscow metro stations are palatial, with polished marble, chandeliers and sculptures. The authorities, evidently regarding station nameboards as unaesthetic, keep the number of signs giving the name of the station to the minimum; for example, there are almost never any names on the platform side of the tracks. So even if you can read Russian you may find it hard, especially in a crowded carriage, to spot a station name to read. However, the names of the stops are always announced over the train's loudspeaker system. Here is a sample of a metro announcement:

Ста́нция Октя́брьская. ... Осторо́жно, две́ри закрыва́ются. Сле́дующая ста́нция Третьяко́вская.
'October Square Station. Careful, the doors are closing. The next station is Tretyakovskaya'.

Buses, trams and trolleybuses also cost five kopecks, but you need a ticket. Conductors are rare and most cities now require you to buy a book of tickets from a kiosk; you can also get them from the driver. <u>You must then validate one of these tickets using one of the metal punches (**компо́стер**) screwed to the wall of the bus.</u> If you can't reach a punch because of the crush, ask the person you're squeezed against to pass your ticket along to somebody who can reach. Say **Переда́йте, пожа́луйста** ('Pass it along, please'). If you want to keep busy during a journey, stand beside a ticket punch on a crowded bus. If you travel without a valid ticket, you may be fined by an inspector **(контроле́р),** usually a harmless-looking old woman disguised in peasant clothes who suddenly reveals an official identity card and a ferocious manner.

To buy tickets in the bus say to the driver: **Кни́жку** [Kne'esh-koo], **пожа́луйста.** He will give you a **кни́жка** (booklet) of ten tickets, costing 50 kopecks.

Taxis

A taxi driver is likely to refuse to take you if he doesn't like your choice of direction. Or he may demand extra money. A packet of Western cigarettes is a relatively cheap way of persuading him to go where you want.

Taxis are always in short supply, and many Russians will simply flag down any passing motorist and agree a price for the journey. You can do the same – just wave that packet of cigarettes with a visible Western brandname.

5 Times and days

Key expressions

When does the museum open?	**Когда́ музе́й открыва́ется?** [Kag-dá moo-zyéy at-kri-vá-ye-tsa?]
When does.it close?	**Когда́ о́н закрыва́ется?** [za-kri-vá-ye-tsa]
(at) one o'clock	**(в) час** [(f) chas]
(at) two o'clock	**(в) два часа́** [(v) dva chee-sá]
(at) five o'clock	**(в) пять часо́в** [(v) pyaty chee-sóf]
this evening	**сего́дня ве́чером** [sye-vód-nya vyé-chye-ram] (Note: here г is pronounced as [v̄])
May I speak to Nina?	**Позови́те, пожа́луйста, Ни́ну** [Pa-za-veé-tye, pa-zhál-sta, Née-noo]
Don't hang up	**Не кла́ди́те тру́бку** [Nye kla-dée-tye tro′op-koo]
Speak slowly, please	**Говори́те ме́дленно, пожа́луйста.** [Ga-va-ree′e-tye myé-dlye-na, pa-zhál-sta]
Do you speak English?	**Вы говори́те по-англи́йски?** [Vi ga-va-ree′e-tye pa-an-glee′e-skee?]
That's agreed/OK	**Договори́лись** [Da-ga-va-ree′e-leesy]

| I'm sorry, it was accidental | **Прости́те, я неча́янно.** [Pra-ste'e-tye, ya nye-chá-ya-na] |
| It doesn't matter | **Ничего́** [Nee-chye-vó] (Note: here г is pronounced as [v]) |

Conversations

1   When does the museum open?

TOURIST   **Когда́ музе́й открыва́ется?**
[Kag-dá moo-zyéy at-kri-vá-ye-tsa?]

GUIDE   **В де́сять часо́в[1].**
[Vdyé-syaty chee-sóf]

2   When does it close?

TOURIST   **Когда́ он[2] закрыва́ется?**
[Kag-dá ón za-kri-vá-ye-tsa?]

GUIDE   **В шесть[1].**
[Fshesty]

3   Is it open every day?

TOURIST   **Музе́й рабо́тает ка́ждый день?**
[Moo-zyéy ra-bó-ta-yet kázh-di dyeny?]

GUIDE   **Ка́ждый день кро́ме понеде́льника.***
[Kázh-di dyeny kró-mye pa-nye-dyély-nee-ka]

*Every day except Monday.

4   You want to be woken in the morning

GUEST   **До́брый ве́чер. Мо́жно[3] меня́ разбуди́ть за́втра в семь часо́в утра́[4]?***
[Dó-bri vyé-chyer. Mózh-na mye-nyá raz-boo-de'ety záf-tra fsyemy chee-sóf oo-trá?]

MAID   **Да, коне́чно, в семь утра́ я вас разбужу́.**** [Da, ka-nyésh-na, fsyemy oo-trá ya vas raz-boo-zho'o]

*Can you wake me tomorrow at 7 am?

**Yes, of course, at 7am I'll wake you. (Note: ч in 'коне́чно' pronounced as [sh])

5   Ordering a taxi

GUEST   **Мо́жно[3] заказа́ть такси́?**

[Mózh-na za-ka-záty tak-see?]

ASSISTANT **Како́е вре́мя?***
[Ka-kó-ye vryé-mya?]

GUEST **Сего́дня ве́чером.**
[Sye-vód-nya vyé-chye-ram]

ASSISTANT **Э-э. Вре́мя то́чное?****
[Vryé-mya tóch-na-ye?]

GUEST **Семь часо́в ве́чера[4].**
[Sycmy chee-sót vyé-chye-ra]

ASSISTANT **Куда́ пое́дете ве́чером?*****
[Koo-dá pa-yé-dye-tye vyé-chye-ram?]

GUEST **В Ки́ровский теа́тр.**
[FKée-raf-skee tye-átr]

ASSISTANT **Так, сто́имость зака́за - пятьдеся́т копе́ек.******
[Tak, stó-ee-masty za-ká-za – pee-dye-syát ka-pyé-yek]

GUEST **Хорошо́.**

*What time?

**The exact time?

***Where will you be going in the evening?

****Right, the order costs fifty kopecks.

6 Arranging a meeting

WOMAN **Приходи́те к нам в понеде́льник[5].***
[Pree-ha-dée-tye knam fpa-nye-dyély-neek]

MAN **В понеде́льник я за́нят. Я могу́ в сре́ду и́ли в пя́тницу[5].***
[Fpa-nye-dyély-neek ya zá-nyat. Ya ma-goó fsryé-doo ée-lee fpyát-nee-tsoo]

WOMAN **Хорошо́. Тогда́ приходи́те[6] в пя́тницу.**
[Ha-ra-shó. Tag-dá pree-ha-dée-tye fpyát-nee-tsoo]
Договори́лись.
[Da-ga-va-rée-leesy]

MAN **Договори́лись.**

*Come and see us on Monday.

**On Monday I'm busy. I can come either on Wednesday or on Friday.

7 Taking down a phone number

MAN 1 **Скажи́те, пожа́луйста, ваш телефо́н.**
[Ska-zhí-tye, pa-zhál-sta, vash tye-lye-fón]

MAN 2 **Пять-во́семь-шесть два-оди́н три-девя́ть.**

MAN 1 **Повтори́те, пожа́луйста.**

MAN 2 **Хорошо́. 5 8 6 2 1 3 9.**

8 Please give that number slowly

MAN **Скажи́те, пожа́луйста, телефо́н Ка́ти*.**
[Ska-zhí-tye, pa-zhál-sta, tye-lye-fón Ká-tee]

WOMAN **Две́сти девяно́сто - со́рок - со́рок четы́ре**

MAN **Пожа́луйста, говори́те ме́дленно. Я иностра́нец.**

WOMAN **Ой, извини́те, пожа́луйста. 290 40 44.**

*Please tell me Katya's telephone number.

9 Ivan Ivanovich isn't in? I'll ring back.

CLERK **Алле́!**
[A-lyó!]

CALLER **Здра́вствуйте, позови́те, пожа́луйста, Ива́на Ива́новича[7].**

CLERK **Его́ нет.***
[Ye-<u>v</u>o nyet]

CALLER **А когда́ он бу́дет?**

CLERK **Он бу́дет че́рез час.****

CALLER **Спаси́бо. Я перезвоню́.**

CLERK **Пожа́луйста.**

*He's out. (Note: г in 'его' is pronounced as [v])
**He'll be here in an hour.

10 Ivan Petrovich isn't back. When will he come?

CLERK **Слу́шаю.**

CALLER **Здра́вствуйте. Позови́те, пожа́луйста, Ива́на Петро́вича[7].**
[Pa-za-veé-tye, pa-zhál-sta, Ee-vá-na Pye-tró-vee-cha]

CLERK **Его́ сего́дня не бу́дет.***
[Ye-vó sye-vód-nya nye boʹo-dyet]

CALLER **Не клади́те, пожа́луйста, тру́бку. А когда́ он придёт?****
[Nye kla-deé-tye, pa-zhál-sta, troʹop-koo. A kag-dá ón pree-dyót?]

CLERK **Óн бýдет тóлько зáвтра. *****
[Ón boó-dyet tóly-ka záf-tra]
CALLER **Спасúбо.**
CLERK **До свидáния.**

*He won't be here today.
**And when will he come?
***He won't be here until tomorrow.

11 Apologising

MAN **Óй!** [Óy!] (Exclamation)
GIRL **Простúте, пожáлуйста, я нечáянно.**
[Pra-stée-tye, pa-zhál-sta, ya nye-chá-ya-na]
MAN **Ничегó, ничегó. Пожáлуйста.**
[Nee-chye-vó, nee-chye-vó]

Word list

аллё [a-lyó]	hello (on phone)
(óн) бýдет	(he) will be
ваш	your
вéчером [vyé-chye-ram]	in the evening
врéмя (n) [vryé-mya]	time
дáйте [dáy-tye]	give
двéсти [dvyé-stee]	two hundred
день (m) [dyeny]	day
зáвтра [záf-tra]	tomorrow
(я) зáнят [ya zá-nyat]	(I'm) busy (man)
(я) занятá [ya za-nee-tá]	(I'm) busy (woman)
заказáть [za-ka-záty]	to order
(музéй) закрывáется [za-kri-vá-ye-tsa]	(the museum) closes
úли	either/or
(я) инострáнец (m) [ya ee-na-strá-nyets]	(I'm) a foreigner (man)
(я) инострáнка (f) [ya ee-na-strán-ka]	(I'm) a foreigner (woman)
кáждый [kázh-di]	every
конéчно [ka-nyésh-na]	of course

кро́ме [kró-mye]	except
куда́ [koo-dá]	(to) where
меня́ [mye-nyá]	me
(я) могу́ [ya ma-goó]	(I) can
ноль [nóly]	zero
(музей) открыва́ется	(the museum) opens
(я) перезвоню́	(I)'ll ring back
[ya pye-rye-zva-nyoó]	
позови́те	call
приходи́те к нам	come and see us
[pree-ha-deé-tye]	(come to us)
(музе́й) рабо́тает	(the museum) works (i.e. is open)
разбуди́ть	to wake
[raz-boo-deéty]	
сего́дня	today
[sye-<u>v</u>ód-nya]	
такси́ (n) [tak-seé]	taxi
телефо́н (m)	telephone/phone number
че́рез час	in an hour
[chyé-ryes chas]	

Explanations

1 Telling the time

The word for 'hour' is **час** [chas], which also means 'o'clock' and 'one o'clock'. After 2, 3 and 4, **час** has the ending **-a**; after 5, 6 etc. the ending is **-ов**:

час	one o'clock/one hour
два часа́ [dva chee-sá]	two o'clock/two hours
три часа́	three o'clock/three hours
семь часо́в	seven o'clock/hours
[syemy chee-sóf]	
де́сять часо́в	ten o'clock/hours

'Minute' is **мину́та** [mee-noó-ta]. After 2, 3 and 4 it becomes **мину́ты** and after 5, 6 etc. **мину́т**:

одна́ мину́та	one minute
две мину́ты	two minutes
де́сять мину́т	ten minutes
три́дцать мину́т	thirty minutes

If you put these two constructions together, you can give any time using the 24-hour clock.

Пятна́дцать часо́в де́сять мину́т: 15.10
This is what you will hear in loudspeaker announcements or on the radio.

To say '*at* a time' simply put **в** ('in', 'at') in front of the time:
в два часа́ at two o'clock

Other useful time phrases:

What time is it?	**Кото́рый час?** [Ka-tó-ri chas?] ('which hour?')
yesterday	**вчера́** [fchye-rá]
in the morning	**у́тром** [óo-tram]

2   He/she/it

All Russian nouns are masculine, feminine or neuter (see page 29). So even when you're talking about *things* rather than about people, you say 'he' (rather than 'it') for masculine nouns and 'she' for feminine nouns.

Музе́й is masculine, so 'it closes' is **он закрыва́ется** ('he'). 'She' (used for feminine nouns such as **у́лица** 'street') is **она́** [a-ná].

'It' is **оно́** [a-nó]. This word is used for neuter nouns, but is not very common.

3   Is it possible?/May I?/Can you?

Мо́жно [mózh-na] covers all three of these. Just find in your dictionary the verb which describes what you want to do, or what you want somebody else to do, and put it after **мо́жно**.

Мо́жно войти́? [Mózh-na vay-tée?] May I come in? (Is it possible to enter?)

Мо́жно меня́ разбуди́ть? [Mózh-na mye-nyá raz-boo-dééty?] Can you wake me? (Is it possible me to wake?)

Мо́жно закури́ть? [Mózh-na za-koo-reéty?] Is it possible to start smoking? (May I smoke?)

Мо́жно заказа́ть такси́? [Mózh-na za-ka-záty tak-seé?] Is it possible to order a taxi?

'You may' is simply **мо́жно.**
'It's not possible' is **нельзя́** [nyely-zyá].

4   am/pm

To say am or pm, the Russians use the following four words:
утра́ [oo-trá] ('of the morning') 4am to midday
дня [dnya] ('of the day') midday to 5 or 6pm
ве́чера [vyé-chye-ra] ('of the evening') 5 or 6 pm
   to midnight
но́чи [nó-chee] ('of the night') midnight to 4am
в семь часо́в ве́чера at 7pm

5   Days of the week (abbreviations in brackets)

Monday	**понеде́льник (пн)** [pa-nye-dyély-neek] по=after+не=not+дел=do–day 'the day after the day you rest'
Tuesday	**вто́рник (вт)** [ftór-neek] 'second day'
Wednesday	**среда́ (ср)** [srye-dá] 'middle day'
Thursday	**четве́рг (чт)** [chyet-vyérk] 'fourth day'
Friday	**пя́тница (пт)** [pyát-nee-tsa] 'fifth day'
Saturday	**суббо́та (сб)** [soo-bó-ta] 'Sabbath'
Sunday	**воскресе́нье (вс)** [vas-krye-syé-nyye] 'resurrection'

To say *on* a particular day, simply use **в** again. With **в**, the three feminine nouns – i.e. the words ending in **-a** – change the ending to **-у**. The words for the other four days, which are masculine (**понеде́льник, вто́рник, четве́рг**) or neuter (**воскресе́нье**), stay the same.

6   Giving instructions

The ordering form (the 'imperative') of most verbs ends **-айте** [-ay-tye] or **-ите** [-ee-tye]. You know examples such as:

Говори́те ме́дленно	Speak slowly
Скажи́те	Tell (me)

To sound polite, just add the word **пожа́луйста.**

Да́йте, пожа́луйста, ко́фе	Please give me a coffee
Напиши́те э́то, пожа́луйста	Write it down, please
Позови́те, пожа́луйста, Ната́шу	Please call Natasha

7 Please call Natasha

Позови́те Ната́шу. Ната́шу is the accusative case of **Ната́ша** after **позови́те** 'call' (see page 43). All names which end in **-a** change to **-y.** And so **Ната́ша** becomes **Ната́шу.** Names of people which end in a consonant, like **Ива́н** or **Влади́мир,** *add* **-a:** so 'Call Ivan Ivanovich' is: **Позови́те Ива́на Ива́новича** [Pa-za-ve'e-tye Ee-vá-na Ee-vá-na-vee-cha].

Exercises

1 Translate into English

(a) Два часа́.
(b) Два́дцать два часа́.
(c) Шесть часо́в три́дцать мину́т.
(d) Музе́й открыва́ется в оди́ннадцать часо́в.
(e) Рестора́н закрыва́ется в двена́дцать часо́в.
(f) В сре́ду.
(g) Приходи́те в пя́тницу и́ли в суббо́ту.
(h) Приходи́те в четве́рг ве́чером.

2 What is the time according to Moscow Radio?
(Моско́вское вре́мя 'Moscow Time')
(a) Моско́вское вре́мя – трина́дцать часо́в.
(b) Моско́вское вре́мя – двена́дцать часо́в одна́ мину́та.

3 Say 'I'll come' (**Я приду́** [Ya pree-do'o])
(a) on Saturday
(b) at three o'clock
(c) in the evening
(d) tomorrow
(e) tomorrow evening

4 What are the working hours of this office?

пн, ср, пт 9-13
вт, чт, сб 14-18

5 Write down the following telephone numbers

(If you have the cassette, try and work out the numbers without looking at the words)

(a) Двести пятьдеся́т шесть – но́ль два – три́дцать пять

(b) Сто́ два́дцать пять – се́мьдесят – девяно́сто де́вять

6 Play the part of the foreigner

FOREIGNER	(Excuse me, when does the Beriozka open?)
RECEPTIONIST	В де́сять.
FOREIGNER	(Repeat please)
RECEPTIONIST	Она́ открыва́ется в де́сять часо́в.
FOREIGNER	(And when does it close?)
RECEPTIONIST	В во́семь часо́в ве́чера.
FOREIGNER	(Thank you)

7 Order a taxi

YOU	(Hello. Can I order a taxi?)
CLERK	Мо́жно. Когда́?
YOU	(This evening)
CLERK	То́чное вре́мя?
YOU	(Eight o'clock)
CLERK	Куда́ пое́дете?
YOU	(To the restaurant Uzbekistan)
CLERK	Хорошо́. С вас пятьдеся́т копе́ек за зака́з.

8 Make a phone call

WOMAN	Да.
YOU	(Can I speak to Natasha, please?)
WOMAN	Её сейча́с нет.
YOU	(Speak slowly, please. I'm a foreigner.)
WOMAN	Её нет. Она́ придёт часо́в в во́семь.
YOU	(Please repeat.)
WOMAN	Она́ придёт в во́семь часо́в.
YOU	(OK, I'll ring back at eight.)

Worth Knowing

Public buildings such as shops, cafés and
museums exhibit notices with their opening hours
in figures – but be warned that all of these,
including shops, are unlikely to admit customers
up to half an hour *before* closing time.

МУЗЕЙ РАБОТАЕТ

Пн	10·00ч – 17·00ч
Вт	— —
Ср	10·00ч – 17·00ч
Чт	10·00ч – 17·00ч
Пт	10·00ч – 17·00ч
Сб	10·00ч – 17·00ч
Вс	10·00ч – 17·00ч

Timetables

Soviet timetables use the twenty-four hour clock.
But note one curious aspect of transport in the
Moscow-centric USSR: despite the eleven time-
zones, all transport timetables use Moscow time
(**Моско́вское вре́мя**), and so do all airport and
station clocks. So you might fly into Irkutsk in
Eastern Siberia at 5 pm according to the timetable
and all the clocks, but outside it's pitch dark.
Locally it's 11 pm – and if you find the restaurant
closed, that's because it works on local time.

Telephoning

Most Russian flats have a phone (**телефо́н**),
and there are plenty of public call boxes (**автома́т**),
from which a call costs only two kopecks. In
addition, your hotel room will almost certainly
contain a direct line telephone and you will not be
charged for local calls. People you meet will
willingly give you their phone numbers, so it is
worth learning the basic phrases for making
contact by phone.

Russians use telephones all the time but they tend
to be abrupt. When answering a call, they say
Да! or **Слу́шаю!** ('I'm listening'), never anything
informative such as their name or number. When
you ring an office number you are likely to find that
if the person you want isn't there, or your request
isn't immediately understood, the phone is banged
down without even **До свида́ния.** So learn the
phrase **Не клади́те тру́бку, пожа́луйста!** [Nye
kla-de'e-tye tro'op-koo, pa-zhál-sta] 'Don't hang up' –
and learn to say it quickly.

6 Socialising

Key expressions

What's your name?	**Как вас зовут?** [Kak vas za-voót?]
My name is...	**Меня зовут...** [Mye-nyá za-voót...]
Pleased to meet you	**Óчень приятно** [Ó-chyeny pree-yát-na]
Your health!	**Ваше здоровье!** [Váshe zda-ró-vyye!]
I like Moscow.	**Мне нравится Москва** [Mnye nrá-vee-tsa Mask-vá]
I don't like...	**Мне не нравится...** [Mnye nye nrá-vee-tsa]
It's very tasty	**Óчень вкусно** [Ó-chyeny fkoó-sna]
I can't eat any more	**Я сыт** [Ya sit] (man) **Я сыта** [si-tá] (woman)
I am (not) married	**Я (не) замужем** (woman) [Ya (nye) zá-moo-zhem] **Я (не) женат** (man) [Ya (nye) zhe-nát]

You will hear:

Познакомьтесь [Pa-zna-kómy-tyesy]	Let me introduce you
Берите [Bye-reé-tye]	Do take some
Налить ещё? [Na-leéty ye-shshyó?]	Can I pour you some more?
Милости просим [Mée-la-stee pró-seem]	Welcome
Раздевайтесь [Raz-dye-váy-tyesy]	Take your coat and shoes off (lit. 'Undress')

Conversations

1 Finding out names

GIRL **Скажи́те, как вас зову́т?**
[Ska-zhí-tye, kak vas za-vóot?]

BOY **Меня́ зову́т Вита́лий. А как вас зову́т?**
[Mye-nyá za-vóot Vee-tá-lee. A kak vas za-vóot?]

GIRL **Меня́ зову́т Мари́я.** [Ma-rée-ya]

2 Asking someone's name

LITTLE GIRL **Скажи́те, пожа́луйста, как вас зову́т?** [Ska-zhí-tye, pa-zhál-sta, kak vas za-vóot?]

WOMAN **Меня́ зову́т Ири́на Влади́мировна[1].**
[Mye-nyá za-vóot Ee-rée-na Vla-dée-mee-rav-na]

3 What are your first name and patronymic?

GIRL **Скажи́те, как ва́ше и́мя и о́тчество[1]?**
[kak vá-she ée-mya ee ó-chye-stva?]

BOY **Вита́лий Григо́рьевич. А как ва́ше и́мя и о́тчество?**

GIRL **Мари́я Арка́дьевна.** [Ar-ká-dyyev-na]

4 Formal introductions

MAN 1 **Меня́ зову́т Алексе́й Эдуа́рдович.**
[A-lyek-syéy E-doo-ár-da-veech]

MAN 2 **О́чень прия́тно.**

MAN 1 **А как зову́т вас?**

MAN 2 **Меня́ зову́т Алекса́ндр Миха́йлович.**
[A-lyek-sándr Mee-háy-la-veech]

MAN 1 **О́чень прия́тно.**

5 Introducing people by first names

MAN **Здра́вствуйте, дороги́е, э́то во́т мо́й брат Семён.* Познако́мьтесь. Э́то Ко́ля.**

SEMYON **О́чень прия́тно.**

MAN **Э́то Фили́ппа.**

*Hello, my friends ('dears'), this is (here) my brother Semyon.

SEMYON	Óчень прия́тно.
MAN	Э́то Ле́на.
SEMYON	Óчень прия́тно.
MAN	Га́ля.

6 Guests arrive

EVERYBODY	Здра́вствуйте!
HOSTESS	Проходи́те. Проходи́те. Раздева́йтесь. Во́т та́почки.
GUESTS	Спаси́бо. Спаси́бо.
HOSTESS	Ми́лости про́сим.

7 Toasts

Мир и сча́стье.* [Meer ee shshá-styye]
Дава́йте вы́пьем за знако́мство[2]. ** [Da-váy-tye ví-pyyem za zna-kóm-stva]
Дава́йте вы́пьем за дру́жбу и мир на земле́.* ** [za dro͡ozh-boo ee meer na zyem-lyé]

*Peace and happiness.
**Let's drink to our meeting.
***Let's drink to friendship and peace on earth.

8 Very tasty

GUEST	Óчень вку́сно! Óчень вку́сно! Про́сто замеча́тельно! [Pró-sta za-mye-chá-tely-na!]
HOSTESS	Ку́шай на здоро́вье.* [Ko͡o-shay na zda-ró-vyye]
GUEST	Спаси́бо. Óчень вку́сно.

*'Eat to your health', a polite reply to praise of food

9 Taking down an address

MAN	Скажи́те, пожа́луйста, где вы[3] живёте?
WOMAN	На Арба́те*: Арба́т, до́м пятна́дцать, кварти́ра семь[4].
MAN	Арба́т, до́м 15, кварти́ра 7.

*On the Arbat, a historic street in central Moscow.

10 A new friend gives her number

GIRL 1 **Мой телефо́н сто́ шестьдеся́т во́семь – пятьдеся́т четы́ре – оди́ннадцать.**

GIRL 2 **Повтори́[3], пожа́луйста, я запишу́.***

GIRL 1 **168 54 11. Позвони́[3] ве́чером, пожа́луйста.**

GIRL 2 **Хорошо́.**

GIRL 1 **До свида́ния.**

GIRL 2 **Пока́.**** [Pa-ká.]

*I'll write (it) down.

**See you (colloquial goodbye).

11 Taking a phone number

GIRL 1 **Мой телефо́н – сто́ пятьдеся́т оди́н – но́ль шесть – но́ль два.**

GIRL 2 **Хорошо́. Я обяза́тельно позвоню́.***

*I'll definitely phone.

12 Arranging to telephone

GIRL 1 **Позвони́те за́втра ве́чером.**

GIRL 2 **А когда́?**

GIRL 1 **В де́вять часо́в.**

GIRL 2 **Хорошо́.**

13 Do you like Leningrad?

GIRL 1 **Вам нра́вится Ленингра́д[5]?**

GIRL 2 **Коне́чно, о́чень нра́вится.**

14 Do you like Moscow?

ADULT **Тебе́ нра́вится[5] Москва́?**

CHILD **Да, о́чень.**

15 Taking leave

GUEST **Спаси́бо вам большо́е, бы́ло о́чень прия́тно.***

HOSTESS **Спаси́бо вам.**

GUEST **К сожале́нию, нам пора́ уходи́ть.****
До за́втра.*** [Ksa-zha-lyé-nee-yoo]

HOSTESS **До свида́ния.**

*it was very nice.

**Unfortunately, it's time for us to leave.

***See you tomorrow (Until tomorrow).

Word list

а́дрес (m)   address
брат (m)   brother
бы́ло   (it) was
ва́ше и́мя (n) [е́e-mya]   your first name
го́род (m) [gó-rat]   city/town
дава́йте вы́пьем   let's drink
до за́втра [da záf-tra]   see you tomorrow
до́м (m)   house/building
дру́жба (f)   friendship
(вы) живёте   (you) live
    [vi zhi-vyó-tye]
замеча́тельно   marvellous
кварти́ра (f)   flat
мир (m)   peace
мир на земле́   peace on earth
мо́й   my
обяза́тельно   definitely
    [a-bee-zá-tyely-na]
о́тчество (n)   patronymic
    [ó-chye-stva]
позвони́те   ring (me)
(я) позвоню́   (I'll) phone
пока́ [pa-ká]   see you soon
прия́тно   pleasant
про́сто   simply
проходи́те   come through
    [pra-ha-de'e-tye]
сча́стье (n) [shshá-styye]   happiness
та́почки (f) [tá-pach-kee]   slippers (nobody wears outdoor shoes at home, and there are always spare pairs for guests)
фами́лия (f) [fa-me'e-lee-ya]   surname

Family relationships
ба́бушка (f) [bá-boosh-ka]   grandmother

брат (m) [brat]		brother
дéдушка (m – despite the -a) [dyé-doosh-ka]		grandfather
дóчь (f) [dóchy]		daughter
женá (f) [zhe-ná]		wife
муж (m) [moosh]		husband
сестрá (f) [sye-strá]		sister
сын (m) [sin]		son

Explanations

1 Names

Every Russian has three names. The first name (**и́мя**) [ée-mya] is a given name, like ours: **Натáлья** [Na-tá-lyya], **Влади́мир** [Vla-dée-meer], **Ивáн** [Ee-ván], **Татья́на** [Ta-tyyá-na], **Михаи́л** [Mee-ha-éel] etc. These first names all have 'intimate' forms, used by friends and family: **Натáша** [Na-tá-sha] from **Натáлья**, **Волóдя** [Va-ló-dya] from **Влади́мир**, **Вáня** [Vá-nya] from **Ивáн**, **Тáня** [Tá-nya] from **Татья́на** etc.

The last name is a surname: **Горбачёв** [Gar-ba-chyóf], **Карéнин** [Ka-ryé-neen]. These surnames are male forms; women add a feminine ending: **Горбачёва** [Gar-ba-chyó-va], **Карéнина** [Ka-ryé-nee-na].

The middle name is formed from the father's first name and is called a patronymic (**óтчество**); men add **-ович** [o-veech/a-veech] to their father's first name: **Ивáнович** [Ee-vá-na-veech], **Влади́мирович** [Vla-dée-mee-ra-veech], while women add **-овна** [ov-na/av-na]: **Ивáновна** [Ee-vá-nav-na], **Влади́мировна** [Vla-dée-mee-rav-na], **Михáйловна** [Mee-háy-lav-na] etc.

Foreigners should know about patronymics for one important reason: when you speak to someone to whom you want to be polite, **Михаи́л Сергéевич Горбачёв** [Mee-ha-éel Syer-gyé-ye-veech Gar-ba-chyóf], for example, you use *his first name and* *patronymic*, and call him **Михаи́л Серге́евич** [Mee-ha-e'el Syer-gyé-ye-veech], which is the equivalent of calling him 'Mr Gorbachev' in English. Russian has no generally used equivalent of Mr/Mrs/Miss/Ms. Even **това́рищ** [ta-vá-reeshsh] 'comrade' is relatively rare and should not be used by foreigners. Learning these double names is hard work to begin with, but your politeness and effort will be appreciated. Try to find out the first name and patronymic of anyone you will have repeated dealings with.

2 Toasts

During alcoholic social occasions, Russians like to begin each round with a different toast (almost the same word in Russian: **то́ст**). The toasts tend to get more and more elaborate as the evening progresses. You will be expected to propose toasts too, so here is a list of simpler ones. Each one starts with the word **за** [za] which literally means 'for'.

Вы́пьем...	Let's drink...
за мир	to peace
за дру́жбу	to friendship
за вас	to you
за на́шу дру́жбу	to our friendship
за а́нгло-сове́тскую дру́жбу	to Anglo-Soviet friendship
за же́нщин	to women

3 You: вы (polite) and ты (familiar)

People you don't know well are addressed as **вы** [vi] ('you') and so is any group of more than one person. To someone you call **вы** you say

Здра́вствуйте [Zdrá-stoovy-tye]	Hello
Прости́те [Pra-ste'e-tye]	Excuse me
Повтори́те [Pa-fta-re'e-tye]	Repeat

A friend, a relative or a child is addressed as **ты** [ti] (like 'tu' in French). The words above lose their **-те** when you speak to someone you call **ты**.

Здра́вствуй [Zdrá-stvooy] Hello
Прости́ [Pra-stée] Excuse me
Повтори́ [Pa-fta-rée] Repeat

4 Russian addresses

Most Russians live in flats, though in the outskirts and in the countryside you will still find the traditional one-family wooden houses with carved windows. A block of flats is a **до́м** [dóm], a word which can also mean 'house' or any building, whether it contains flats or offices or shops. Each **до́м** has a number, but take note that the same number may cover several buildings, usually one behind the other; each of these same-numbered buildings is called a **ко́рпус** ('block'). If you are given a private address, it may look like this:

Москва́ (+six-figure postcode)
у́лица Го́рького
до́м 6, ко́рпус 2, кварти́ра 153
Ивано́ву Н.Н.

Gorky Street, building no. 6, block no. 2, flat 153, *to* Mr N.N. Ivanov (with the surname in a form called the dative case). The words **до́м** etc. are often omitted, but the house, block and flat number are always given in that order, i.e. 6/2/153. The city always comes first and the resident's name last.

5 I like the flat

'I like' is **Мне нра́вится** (literally 'To me pleases...'). Just add the word for whatever it is you like: 'flat' is **кварти́ра**. So **Мне нра́вится кварти́ра.**

The question 'Do you like Moscow?' is **Вам нра́вится Москва́?** ('To you pleases Moscow?')

If you're talking to someone you know well – someone you would call **ты** – **вам** changes to **тебе́**:

Тебе́ нра́вится Москва́?

Exercises

1 Say in Russian
(a) My name is ... (fill in your name)
(b) What is your name?

2 What are the names of the people?
(a) Меня зову́т Ири́на Никола́евна.
(b) Меня зову́т Татья́на Алекса́ндровна.

3 Play the part of the foreigner
YOUR FRIEND	Познако́мьтесь. Это моя́ жена́ Ве́ра.
YOU	(Pleased to meet you)
VERA	Вам нра́вится Москва́?
YOU	(Very much)

4 Play the part of the guest
HOST	Нали́ть вам ещё?
YOU	(Please do *or* No thank you)
HOST	Бери́те ещё.
YOU	(No thank you, I'm full)
HOST	Бери́те, бери́те.
YOU	(Thank you, I can't)

5 To what and whom is this Russian (recorded in a Leningrad - Moscow sleeper) raising his glass? (**наро́д** means 'people')
Мы вы́пьем за на́шу дру́жбу, мы вы́пьем за англи́йский наро́д.

6 Propose one or all of these toasts
YOUR HOST	За что́ вы́пьем?
YOU	(To peace/to friendship/to Anglo-Soviet friendship/to you/to us/to Gorbachev)

Worth knowing

Meeting Russians at home
Russians in big cities tend to be short of space (two rooms for a family of three is common) and they may be nervous about inviting you to their rather cramped flats. However, if you make it clear that you would love to visit a Russian home, they

are usually happy to oblige. Socialising at home, often in the kitchen, is very much part of Russian life – there are no pubs, beer bars are often sordid, cafés are scarce, and restaurants, with their loud bands and relatively high prices, are for dancing and drinking rather than talking.

If the invitation is made a day or two in advance, you can expect to be served a full-scale meal in the main room of the flat and the hosts will have spent most of the day preparing it (and who knows how long finding the ingredients). Here you will find good traditional Russian cooking of a kind that is simply not provided in hotels or the main restaurants: various kinds of marinated mushrooms, elaborate salads, rich soup in which you can stand a spoon upright. The whole evening will be spent round the dining table and the meal will not be a rushed affair.

If the invitation is issued on the spot, you will probably sit round the kitchen table and the hosts will bring out everything they happen to have in the flat, which will probably be bread **(хлеб)**, cold sausage **(колбасá)** and cheese **(сыр)**, perhaps some pickled cabbage **(капýста)** or mushrooms **(грибы́)**, and tea **(чай).** Russians do not normally keep alcohol at home: it is bought for each occasion, and no bottle is ever left unfinished (most Russian vodka bottles have tear-off tops, and, once opened, they *cannot* be closed). So take a bottle of vodka from your hotel Beriozka. Take other things too (see the presents section opposite). Presents, particularly from foreigners, are very much appreciated.

When you enter, you should take off your shoes. **Тáпочки** [tá-pach-kee] 'slippers' will be provided. Then you will be offered the chance to **помы́ть рýки** [pa-míty ro'o-kee] 'wash your hands'. In modern Russian flats, the toilet and bathroom are separate small windowless rooms side by side; the toilet is normally the door on the right.

One of the first things you will be asked is, 'Are you married?' Russian has different words for saying whether men and women are married. A woman is **за́мужем** [zá-moo-zhem] (lit. 'behind a husband'); a man is **жена́т** [zhe-nát] 'wifed'.

Вы за́мужем? Are you married?
Нет, не за́мужем. No, I'm not.

Presents for Russians

Meeting Russians is not difficult: they want to meet you. So take plenty of presents. One consequence of the shortage of consumer goods is that choosing presents is easy. Go round to your local supermarket and stock up on jars of instant coffee, tins of tea, anything nicely packaged (plastic carrier bags also make popular presents, especially if they are decorated with shop names or advertising material). Cosmetics are always welcome, as are blank cassettes, any kind of clothing (preferably with a Western brand name), books in English (modern novels), calculators, batteries (for calculators and personal stereos), biscuits or sweets in attractive jars or tins which can be used as exotic food containers after the contents have been distributed.

Can you 'Get By'?

Where there are several possible answers give the simplest.

Read and translate these signs

1) РЕСТОРА́Н
2) ТАКСИ́
3) ВЫ́ХОД
4) КО́ФЕ НЕТ
5) У́ЛИЦА ГО́РЬКОГО

Basic contacts

6) Say 'Hello'.
7) Say 'Goodbye'.
8) Say 'Thank you'.
9) Say 'Excuse me'.
10) Say 'Thank you very much'.

Buying things

11) Ask how much it costs.
12) Say 'Three, please.'
13) Ask the assistant to show it to you.
14) Ask for two coffees.
15) Say 'Give me two postcards, please.'

How much is it?

16) Пять рубле́й.
17) Два рубля́ де́сять копе́ек.
18) Два́дцать рубле́й три́дцать шесть копе́ек.
19) Девяно́сто три копе́йки.
20) Со́рок де́вять рубле́й.

Asking for things in restaurants

21) Ask if there is tea.
22) Say 'What have you got?'
23) Ask for coffee without sugar.

24) Ask for mineral water.
25) Ask the waiter to bring the bill.

Getting around

26) Ask where the underground is.
27) Ask how to get there by transport.
28) Ask the passenger next to you to pass your **талóн** along to the ticket punch.
29) Ask the passenger in front of you if he is getting off.
30) Say 'Excuse me, where do I get off?'

Getting things done

31) Ask when the post-office (**пóчта**) opens.
32) Say 'Speak slowly, please.'
33) Say 'Do you speak English?'
34) Ask if you can order a taxi to the Bolshoy Theatre.
35) Say on the phone 'May I speak to Natasha?'

Work out the following times, days and telephone number

36) Приходи́те в семь часо́в.
37) Девятна́дцать часо́в три́дцать мину́т.
38) В сре́ду и в пя́тницу.
39) Ива́н Ива́нович бу́дет в четве́рг, у́тром.
40) Стó два́дцать три - шестьдеся́т вóсемь - нóль четы́ре.

Social encounters

41) Reply to Как вас зову́т?
42) Say 'Pleased to meet you.'
43) Say 'I like Moscow (*or* Leningrad *or* the flat *or* Natasha) very much.'
44) Say 'Thank you. It was very tasty.'
45) Say 'Please give me your address (*or* telephone number).'

Answers to the exercises and test

Introduction

1 [spa-sée-ba] (Remember to pronounce unstressed
   o as [a])
   [dva kó-fye]
   [chye-tí-rye]
   [ya slóo-sha-yoo]
   [Gdye moo-zyéy?]
   [ma-ró-zhe-na-ye]
   [É-ta ha-ra-shó]
   [ón pree-dyót]
   [ta-vá-reeshsh]
   [dvye-ná-tsaty] (second **д** not audible)

2 **Signs:** [BAR] [BOO-FYÉT] [GA-STÉE-NEE-TSA]
   [ZA-KRÍ-TA] [ZÁ-NYA-TA] [ZA-PRYE-SHSHYE-NÓ]
   [EEN-TOO-RÉEST] [KÁ-SSA] [KSYE-BYÉ]
   [MYÉ-STA DLYA KOO-RYÉ-NEE-YA]
   [NYE KOO-RÉETY] [AT SYE-BYÁ]
   [PA-REEK-MÁ-HYER-SKA-YA] [PÓCH-TA]
   [RAZ-MYÉN] [RYE-MÓNT] [RYE-STA-RÁN]
   [SVA-BÓD-NA] [STÓP] [STA-YÁN-KA TAK-SÉE]
   [TOO-A-LYÉT]

Unit 1

1 (a) [A-E-RA-FLÓT]
   (b) [VÓT-KA]
   (c) [EEN-TOO-RÉEST]
   (d) [KEE-ÓSK]
   (e) [LYE-NEEN-GRÁT]
   (f) [MASK-VÁ]
   (g) [PÉP-SEE-KÓ-LA]
   (h) [PRÁV-DA]

2 Здра́вствуйте, Ива́н Петро́вич.
   [Zdrá-stvooy-tye]

3 Здра́вствуй, Са́ша.
[Zdrá-stvooy]

4 Здра́вствуйте. Три ко́фе, пожа́луйста.
[Tree kó-fye, pa-zhál-sta]
Спаси́бо.
[Spa-seé-ba]

Оди́н чай, пожа́луйста.
[A-deén chay, pa-zhál-sta]
Спаси́бо.

5 (a) [a-deén], [dva], [tree], [chay], [kó-fye],
[chye-ti-rye], [spa-seé-ba], [pa-zhál-sta],
[Dó-bri dyeny], [Dó-bra-ye oó-tra],
[Da svee-dá-nee-ya], [Zdrá-stvooy-tye]

(b) [Mask-vá], [vót-ka], [Lón-dan], [Chay-kóf-skee],
[Da-sta-yéf-skee]

(c) Tolstoy (Толсто́й), Gorbachev (Горбачёв),
Pasternak (Пастерна́к), Solzhenitsyn
(Солжени́цын), Khrushchev (Хрущёв), Pushkin
(Пу́шкин), Prokofiev (Проко́фьев).

Unit 2

1 Five roubles.

2 Forty kopecks.

3 (a) Ско́лько сто́ит?
(b) Три, пожа́луйста.
(c) Два рубля́ де́сять копе́ек, пожа́луйста.

4 Ско́лько сто́ит (одна́) откры́тка?
Две, пожа́луйста.
Спаси́бо.

5 Ско́лько сто́ят я́блоки?
(А за) во́семь (рубле́й)?
Де́сять.
Хорошо́, оди́ннадцать.
Оди́н килогра́мм/Одно́ кило́.

6 Forty-four kopecks.

7 Sixty-six kopecks.

8 (a) Cashdesk
(b) Apples 5 roubles a kilo
(c) One postcard – 6 kopecks

Unit 3

1 Mineral water – no. Vodka – no. Black coffee – yes.
White coffee – no. Pepsi – no. Lemonade – yes.
(**сего́дня** 'today'; **у нас во́дки не быва́ет** 'we
don't sell vodka')

2 A small coffee with sugar. (**Я возьму́ ча́шку** [Ya
vazy-moo chásh-koo] means 'I'll take a cup')

3 10 roubles 40 kopecks.

4 Официа́нт, счёт, пожа́луйста.
Повтори́те, пожа́луйста.

5 (a) 8 roubles 30 kopecks
   (b) 50 kopecks
   (c) 3 roubles 15 kopecks
   (d) 12 roubles 86 kopecks

6 Прости́те, ко́фе есть/есть ко́фе?
Во́дка есть?
Чай есть?
Что́ (же) у вас есть?
Минера́льная вода́, пожа́луйста.
Две, пожа́луйста. (буты́лка is feminine)

Unit 4

1 (a) on/to the right
   (b) on/to the left
   (c) straight on
   (d) (You have to) go (travel) three stops.

2 Прости́те, где метро́?
Где остано́вка?
Спаси́бо.

3 (a) Прости́те (*or* Скажите), пожа́луйста, где
   гости́ница Росси́я?
   (b) Прости́те, где метро́?
   (c) Прости́те, как пройти́ в Большо́й теа́тр?
   (d) Прости́те, как прое́хать туда́?

4 Прости́те, где Кра́сная пло́щадь?
It's round the corner and straight on along the
street.

5 Нет (не выхожу́).
You should get out of the way.

6 Прости́те, где Эрмита́ж?
Прости́те, я не понима́ю. Повтори́те,

пожа́луйста.
А как прое́хать туда́?
Повтори́те, пожа́луйста.
Спаси́бо.

Unit 5

1 (a) Two o'clock/Two hours
   (b) 10pm (2200 hours)/Twenty-two hours
   (c) 6.30
   (d) The museum opens at 11.
   (e) The restaurant closes at 12.
   (f) On Wednesday
   (g) Come on Friday or Saturday.
   (h) Come on Thursday evening.

2 (a) 1300 (1pm)
   (b) 1201

3 (a) в суббо́ту
   (b) в три часа́
   (c) ве́чером
   (d) за́втра
   (e) за́втра ве́чером

4 M/W/F   9 a.m. – 1 p.m.
   Tu/Th/Sa   2 p.m. – 6 p.m.

5 (a) 256-02-35
   (b) 125-70-99

6 Прости́те (Скажи́те), пожа́луйста, когда́
   открыва́ется Берёзка?
   Повтори́те, пожа́луйста.
   А когда́ она́ (feminine) закрыва́ется?
   Спаси́бо.

7 Здра́вствуйте. Мо́жно заказа́ть такси́?
   Сего́дня ве́чером.
   Во́семь часо́в.
   В рестора́н Узбекиста́н.

8 Позови́те, пожа́луйста, Ната́шу.
   (She's not here at the moment.)
   Говори́те ме́дленно, пожа́луйста. Я
   иностра́нец/иностра́нка.
   (She's not here. She'll come about eight.)
   Повтори́те, пожа́луйста.
   (She'll come at eight o'clock.)
   Хорошо́, я перезвоню́ в во́семь (часо́в).

Unit 6

1 (a) Меня́ зову́т...
  (b) Как вас зову́т?
2 (a) Irina Nikolaevna [Ee-reé-na Nee-ka-lá-yev-na]
  (b) Tatyana Aleksandrovna [Ta-tyyá-na A-lyek-sán-drav-na]
3 Óчень прия́тно.
  Óчень.
4 Пожа́луйста *or* Нет, спаси́бо.
  Нет, спаси́бо, я сыт(á).
  Спаси́бо, (я) не могу́.
5 To our friendship, to the English (British) people.
6 За мир/за дру́жбу/за англо-сове́тскую дру́жбу/
  за вас/за нас/за Горбачёва (accusative case –
  see Unit 5 note 7).

'Can you get by?'

1) [RYE-STA-RÁN] RESTAURANT
2) [TAK-SEÉ] TAXI
3) [VÍ-HAT] EXIT
4) [KÓ-FYE NYET] NO COFFEE
5) [ÓO-LEE-TSA GÓRY-KA-VA] GORKY STREET
6) Здра́вствуйте.
7) До свида́ния.
8) Спаси́бо.
9) Прости́те.
10) Спаси́бо большо́е.
11) Ско́лько (э́то) сто́ит?
12) Три, пожа́луйста.
13) Покажи́те (э́то), пожа́луйста.
14) Два ко́фе, пожа́луйста.
15) (Да́йте) две откры́тки, пожа́луйста.
16) 5 roubles.
17) 2 roubles 10 kopecks.
18) 20 roubles 36 kopecks.
19) 93 kopecks.
20) 49 roubles.
21) Чай есть?

22) Чтó у вас есть?
23) Кóфе без сáхара, пожáлуйста.
24) Минерáльная водá, пожáлуйста.
25) (Официáнт), счёт, пожáлуйста.
26) (Простúте), где метрó?
27) Как проéхать тудá?
28) Передáйте талóн, пожáлуйста.
29) Вы выхóдите?
30) Простúте, где (мне) выходúть?
31) Когдá открывáется пóчта?
32) Говорúте мéдленно, пожáлуйста.
33) Вы говорúте по-англúйски?
34) Мóжно заказáть таксú в Большóй теáтр?
35) Позовúте, пожáлуйста, Натáшу.
36) Come at 7.
37) 1930 (7.30pm).
38) On Wednesday and Friday.
39) Ivan Ivanovich will be (here) on Thursday, in the morning.
40) 123-68-04.
41) Меня́ зовýт (your name).
42) Óчень прия́тно.
43) Мне óчень нрáвится Москвá/Ленингрáд/квартúра/Натáша.
44) Спасúбо. Бы́ло óчень вкýсно.
45) Дáйте (or Скажúте), пожáлуйста, ваш áдрес/телефóн.

Word list (Russian-English)

Quick reference alphabet in dictionary order

А	Б	В	Г	Д	Е	Ё	Ж	З	И	Й	К	Л	М	Н	О	П	Р
а	б	в	г	д	е	ё	ж	з	и	й	к	л	м	н	о	п	р
a	b	v	g	d	ye	yo	zh	z	ee	y	k	l	m	n	o	p	r

С	Т	У	Ф	Х	Ц	Ч	Ш	Щ	Ъ	Ы	Ь	Э	Ю	Я
с	т	у	ф	х	ц	ч	ш	щ	ъ	ы	ь	э	ю	я
s	t	oo	f	h	ts	ch	sh	shsh	–	i	y	e	yoo	ya

This vocabulary list gives all the vocabulary used in the conversations and exercises. The number shows the unit in which the word first occurs. Pronunciation is shown only when there is some exceptional feature

а 2	*but/and*
автобус 4	*bus*
áдрес 6	*address*
аллё! 5	*hello (on phone)*
английский 6	*English/British*
Áнглия 2	*England/Britain*
апельсиновый сок 3	*orange juice*
аспирин 1	*aspirin*
бáбушка 6	*grandmother*
без 3	*without*
без сáхара 3	*without sugar*
бéлое винó 3	*white wine*
берите 6	*do take some*
билéт 2	*ticket*
большóй 3	*large, big*
бóрщ 3	*beetroot soup*
брат 6	*brother*
(óн) бýдет 5	*(he) will (be)*
(вы) бýдете 3	*(you) will*
бýдьте добры 3	*be so good/excuse me*
бутербрóд 3	*open sandwich*
бутербрóд с сыром 3	*cheese sandwich*
бутылка 3	*bottle*
было 6	*(it) was*
в 4/5	*in/to/at*
вам 3	*to you/for you*
вас 1	*you (accusative of вы)*

ваш 5	your
ва́ше 6	your
ва́ше здоро́вье! 6	your health!
ва́ши 2	your (plural of ваш)
вегетариа́нец 3	vegetarian
ве́чер 1	evening
ве́чером 5	in the evening
вино́ 3	wine
вку́сно 6	tasty
вода́ 3	water
во́дка 3	vodka
во́семь 2	eight
во́семьдесят 2	eighty
воскресе́нье 5	Sunday
во́т 2	here/there (pointing)
вре́мя 5	time
всего́ [fsye-vó] 2	altogether/in all
вто́рник 5	Tuesday
второ́е блю́до 3	second (main) course
вхо́д 4	entrance
вчера́ 5	yesterday
вы 3	you
вы́пить 3	to drink (alcohol)
вы́ход 4	exit
(вы) выхо́дите 4	(you) are getting out
выходи́ть 4	to get out
(я) выхожу́ 4	(I) am getting out
где 4	where
(вы) говори́те 5	(you) speak
говори́те ме́дленно 5	speak slowly
го́род 6	city/town
гру́ши 2	pears
да 2	yes
дава́йте вы́пьем 6	let's drink
да́йте 5	give (me)
далеко́ 4	far
два 1	two
два́дцать 2	twenty
двена́дцать 2	twelve
две́сти 5	two hundred
девяно́сто 2	ninety
де́вять 2	nine
де́душка 6	grandfather
день 5	day
десе́рт 3	dessert
де́сять 2	ten
для 3	for
для вас 3	for you
до 4	as far as/until

до за́втра 6	see you tomorrow
до свида́ния 1	goodbye
добра́ться [da-brá-tsa] 4	to reach/get to
до́брый 1	good/kind
договори́лись 5	that's agreed/OK
до́м 6	house/building
дороги́е 6	(my) dears
до́рого 2	expensive
до́чь 6	daughter
дру́жба 6	friendship
его́ [ye-vó] 5	him/of him
её 5	her/of her
(я) ем 3	(I) eat
е́сли 2	if
есть 3	to eat
есть 3	is/are
есть? 3	is there?
ещё раз 2	again
жена́ 6	wife
жена́т 6	married (of man)
(вы) живёте 6	(you) live
за 2	for
за знако́мство 6	to our meeting
за нас 6	to us
за угло́м 4	round the corner
за́втра 5	tomorrow
за́втра у́тром 5	tomorrow morning
зака́з 5	order
заказа́ть 5	to order
закрыва́ется 5	closes
замеча́тельно 6	marvellous
за́мужем 6	married (of woman)
за́нят 5	busy (man)
занята́ 5	busy (woman)
(я) запишу́ 6	(I')ll write (it) down
здесь 4	here
здоро́вье 6	health
здра́вствуй 1	hello (informal)
здра́вствуйте 1	hello
(вы) зна́ете 4	(you) know
(я) зна́ю 3	(I) know
зову́т 6	(they) call
и 2	and
извини́те 4	excuse (me)
и́ли 3	either/or
и́мя 6	first name
иностра́нец 5	foreigner (man)
иностра́нка 5	foreigner (woman)

к нам 5	*to us*
к сожалéнию 6	*unfortunately*
кáждый 5	*every*
как 4	*how*
как вас зовýт? 6	*what's your name?*
как проéхать ...? 4	*How do I get to ... (by transport)?*
как пройти...? 4	*How do I get to... (on foot)?*
какóй 3	*what kind of*
кáсса 2	*cash desk/ticket office*
квартúра 6	*flat*
килó 2	*kilo*
килогрáмм 2	*kilogram*
Кúровский теáтр 4	*the Kirov Theatre*
когдá 4	*when*
колбасá 3	*salami*
конвéрт 2	*envelope*
конéчно 5 [ka-nyésh-na]	*of course*
копéйка 2	*kopeck*
кóрпус 6	*block*
кóфе 1	*coffee*
Крáсная плóщадь 4	*Red Square*
крáсное винó 3	*red wine*
крóме 5	*except*
кудá 5	*(to) where*
лýчше [lóo-che] 4	*better*
мáленький 3	*small*
мéдленно 5	*slowly*
меню́ 3	*menu*
меня́ 5	*me*
меня́ зовýт... 6	*my name is...*
метрó 4	*metro/underground*
мúлости прóсим 6	*welcome*
минерáльная водá 3	*mineral water*
минýта 5	*minute*
мир 6	*peace*
мир на землé 6	*peace on earth*
мне 2	*for me/to me*
мне нáдо 4	*I have to*
(я) могý 5	*(I) can*
мóжно 2	*it's possible*
мой 6	*my*
морóженое 3	*ice cream*
муж 6	*husband*
музéй 4	*museum*
на 4	*on/to*
на вторóе 3	*for the main course*
на десéрт 3	*for dessert*
на здорóвье 6	*may it do you good*

на́до 4	it is necessary
нале́во 4	on/to the left
нали́ть ещё? 6	can I pour some more?
напра́во 4	on/to the right
на́ша 6	our
не 3	not
не́ за что 4	don't mention it
не клади́те тру́бку 5	don't hang up
не нра́вится... 6	I don't like...
недалеко́ 4	not far
нельзя́ 5	it's not possible
нет 2	no
нет 3	there is no
не́ту (colloquial) 3	there is no
неча́янно 5	accidentally
ничего́ [nee-chye-vó] 5	it doesn't matter
ноль 5	zero
но́мер 4	number
нра́вится 6	(it) pleases
обяза́тельно 6	definitely
о́вощи 3	vegetables
оди́н 1	one
оди́ннадцать 2	eleven
одну́ мину́ту 3	just a minute
о́й! 2	oh!
о́н 4	he
она́ 5	she
остано́вка 4	stop
открыва́ется 5	opens
откры́тка 2	postcard
отсю́да 4	from here
о́тчество 6	patronymic
официа́нт 3	waiter/waitress
о́чень 2	very/very much
о́чень прия́тно 6	pleased to meet you
переда́йте 4	pass (this) along
(я) перезвоню́ 5	(I')ll ring back
пи́во 3	beer
письмо́ 2	letter
пить 3	to drink
пло́щадь 4	square
по 4	along
по у́лице 4	along the street
по-англи́йски 5	in English
повтори́ 6	repeat (familiar)
повтори́те 2	repeat
(вы) пое́дете 5	(you) will go
пожа́луйста 1	please/don't mention it/please do/here you are

позвони́те 6	ring/telephone
(я) позвоню́ 6	(I')ll phone
познако́мьтесь 6	let me introduce you
позови́те 5	call
пока́ 6	see you soon
покажи́те 2	show (me)
понеде́льник 5	Monday
(я) понима́ю 5	(I) understand
(нам) пора́ уходи́ть 6	it's time (for us) to go
посла́ть 2	to send
по́чта 4	post office
(о́н) придё́т 5	(he) will come
(я) принесу́ 3	(I')ll bring
приходи́те 5	come
прия́тно 6	pleasant
проспе́кт 4	avenue
прости́те 1	excuse (me)
про́сто 6	simply
проходи́те 6	come/go through
пря́мо 4	straight on
пя́тница 5	Friday
пять 2	five
пятьдеся́т 2	fifty
рабо́тает 5	works
разбуди́ть 5	to wake
(я вас) разбужу́ 5	(I')ll wake (you)
раздева́йтесь 6	take off your coat
рубль 2	rouble
ру́сский 4	Russian
ры́ба 3	fish
ря́дом 4	nearby/alongside
с 3	with
с вас 3	from you/you owe
сади́тесь 4	get in/sit down
самолё́том 2	by plane
са́хар 3	sugar
сего́дня 5 [sye-vód-nya]	today
сего́дня ве́чером 5	this evening
сейча́с 5	now/right now
семь 2	seven
се́мьдесят 2	seventy
сестра́ 6	sister
сесть 4	to sit/take transport
скажи́те 2	tell (me)
ско́лько 2	how much/how many
ско́лько сто́ит? 2	how much does it cost?
ско́лько сто́ят? 2	how much do they cost
сле́дующая остано́вка 4	the next stop
(я) слу́шаю 1	I'm listening
со́к 3	juice

со́рок 2	forty
спаси́бо 1	thank you
спаси́бо большо́е 2	thank you very much
среда́ 5	Wednesday
сто́ 2	hundred
сто́имость зака́за 5	the cost of the order
сто́ит 2	costs
Столи́чная во́дка 2	Stolichnaya vodka
суббо́та 5	Saturday
сухо́е вино́ 3	dry wine
сча́стье [shsha-styye] 6	happiness
счёт [shshyot] 3	bill
сын 6	son
сыр 3	cheese
(я) сыт (man) 6	I can't eat any more
(я) сыта́ (woman) 6	I can't eat any more
так 2	so
такси́ 4	taxi
тало́н 4	travel coupon/ticket
та́почки 6	slippers
теа́тр 4	theatre
телефо́н 5	telephone/phone number
това́рищ 6	comrade
тогда́ 3	then
то́же 3	too
то́лько 3	only
то́чное вре́мя 5	exact time
трамва́й 4	tram
три 1	three
три́дцать 2	thirty
тролле́йбус 4	trolleybus
тру́бка 5	receiver
туда́ 4	(to) there
ты 6	you (familiar)
у вас 3	you have
у вас есть...? 3	have you got...?
у́лица 4	street
у́лица Го́рького 4 [-ka-va]	Gorky Street
у́тро 1	morning
у́тром 5	in the morning
(я) хочу́ 2	(I) want
фами́лия 6	surname
хорошо́ 2	good/well/OK
чай 1	tea
час 5	hour
че́рез час 5	in an hour
четве́рг 5	Thursday

четы́ре 1	four
что 3 [shtó]	what
что же 3 [shtó zhe]	what (more emphatic)
шесть 2	six
шестьдеся́т 2	sixty
Эрмита́ж 4	the Hermitage
э́то 2	this/that/it
я 1	I
я́блоки 2	apples

Selected English-Russian phrase list

Does anyone here speak English?	**Кто здесь говори́т по-англи́йски?** [Któ zdyesy ga-va-ре́et pa-an-gle͠e-skee?]
Doctor	**До́ктор** [Dók-tar]
Excuse me	**Прости́те** [Pra-ste͠e-tye]
Go away	**Уходи́те** [Oo-ha-de͠e-tye]
Help me, please	**Помоги́те, пожа́луйста** [Pa-ma-ge͠e-tye, pa-zhál-sta]
Repeat, please	**Повтори́те, пожа́луйста** [Pa-fta-re͠e-tye, pa-zhál-sta]
Write it down please	**Напиши́те, пожа́луйста** [Na-pee-shi-tye, pa-zhál-sta]
I'm English	**Я англича́нин** (man) [Ya an-glee-chá-neen]
	англича́нка (woman) an-glee-chán-ka]
Irish	**ирла́ндец** (man) eer-lán-dyets]
	ирла́ндка (woman) eer-lánt-ka]
Scottish	**шотла́ндец** (man) shat-lán-dyets]
	шотла́ндка (woman) shat-lánt-ka]
Welsh	**валли́ец** (man) va-le͠e-yets]
	валли́йка (woman) va-le͠e-ka]

Further study

Dictionary

A very good and inexpensive dictionary is *The Pocket Oxford Russian-English English-Russian Dictionary*, Oxford University Press, 1981.

Further study

If you want to study Russian in more detail, including all the basic grammar, there is N.J. Brown, *Russian in Three Months*, Hugo's Language Books, 1988. A more demanding course, up to first examination level, is Harrison, Clarkson and Le Fleming, *Colloquial Russian*, Routledge, 1973.

The Centre for Information on Language Teaching (CILT) has information on all the Russian teaching materials in print in Britain. Their offices and library are at Regent's College, Inner Circle, Regent's Park, London NW1 4NS. Tel: 01-486 8221.